Writing the Sacred into the Real

THE CREDO SERIES

A *credo* is a statement of belief, an assertion of deep conviction. The *Credo* series offers contemporary American writers whose work emphasizes the natural world and the human community the opportunity to discuss their essential goals, concerns, and practices. Each volume presents an individual writer's *credo*, his or her investigation of what it means to write about human experience and society in the context of the more-than-human world, as well as a biographical profile and complete bibliography of the author's published work. The *Credo* series offers some of our best writers an opportunity to speak to the fluid and subtle issues of rapidly changing technology, social structure, and environmental conditions.

Writing the Sacred
into the Real

Alison Hawthorne Deming

Scott Slovic, *Credo* Series Editor

Credo

MILKWEED EDITIONS

Published 2001 by Milkweed Editions
Printed in Canada
Cover photo by Beth Olson
Cover design by Sally Wagner
Author photo by Alden Borders
The text of this book is set in Stone Serif.
01   02   03   04   05   5   4   3   2   1
First Edition

Milkweed Editions, a nonprofit publisher, gratefully acknowledges support from our World As Home funders: Lila-Wallace Reader's Digest Fund and Reader's Legacy underwriter Elly Sturgis. Other support has been provided by the Elmer L. and Eleanor J. Andersen Foundation; James Ford Bell Foundation; Bush Foundation; General Mills Foundation; Honeywell Foundation; Jerome Foundation; McKnight Foundation; Minnesota State Arts Board through an appropriation by the Minnesota State Legislature; Norwest Foundation on behalf of Norwest Bank Minnesota, Norwest Investment Management and Trust, Lowry Hill, Norwest Investment Services, Inc.; Lawrence and Elizabeth Ann O'Shaughnessy Charitable Income Trust in honor of Lawrence M. O'Shaughnessy; Oswald Family Foundation; Ritz Foundation on behalf of Mr. and Mrs. E. J. Phelps Jr.; John and Beverly Rollwagen Fund of the Minneapolis Foundation; St. Paul Companies, Inc.; Star Tribune Foundation; Dayton's Project Imagine with support from Target Foundation; U.S. Bancorp Piper Jaffray Foundation on behalf of U.S. Bancorp Piper Jaffray; and generous individuals.

Library of Congress Cataloging-in-Publication Data

Deming, Alison Hawthorne, 1946–
    Writing the sacred into the real / Alison Hawthorne Deming.—1st ed.
        p. cm. — (Credo)
    Includes bibliographical references.
    ISBN 1-57131-248-X (cloth) — ISBN 1-57131-249-8 (pbk.)
        1. Deming, Alison Hawthorne, 1946– 2. Poets, American—20th century—Biography. 3. Poetry—Authorship. 4. Holy, The. 5. Nature. I. Title II. Credo series (Minneapolis, Minn.)

PS3554.E474 Z477 2001
811'.54—dc21
[B]   00-048996

This book is printed on acid-free, recycled paper.

To all the writers,
living and dead, who have shaped
my faith in human culture.

Writing the Sacred into the Real

Above all, the world exists, it is there, and it has a structure; it is not a chaos but a cosmos, hence it presents itself as creation, as work of the gods.

—Mircea Eliade

To be in any form, what is that?

—Walt Whitman

Writing the Sacred
into the Real

Writing the Sacred into the Real

by Alison Hawthorne Deming

Preface

From my upstairs study window, I watch my neighbor come and go. He leaves home in his pickup early in the morning, carrying a thermos of coffee. He drives down to the wharf, mends twine, or paints the wheelhouse on the seiner, or tinkers with the engine. Perhaps he goes to tend the vegetable garden that he grows at his mother's house down the road, mending nets there too to save his crops from the crows. At noon he drives back into the driveway, takes the empty thermos indoors, tells his wife what work got done and what is left to do after lunch. His work is clear to him. He rises to it each day.

I rise to my work each day. I start out in the morning with an idea, and I try to get it onto the page. The idea turns into a bead of mercury, breaks up, and scatters. I sit. I drink coffee. I stare at my neighbor's empty driveway, at the spruce trees between our houses, one so laden with fertile cones I'm surprised it has the energy to breathe. The tree overdoes it. Which cones will sprout into seedlings? The tree has no favorites. Circumstance will decide.

I return to the page, and the skittering splatter of mercury.

The rain is falling in silver needles into the forest green outside my window. The wind slathers it against the glass and it smears into little lenses of distorting clarity. Some raindrops gather on the window casing, bead up fat and round, then fall. The rain's forms are all beautiful. The human eye does more than see; it stitches the seen and unseen together, the temporal and the eternal. It wakes me again and again to the astonishment of finding myself in a body moving through a world of beauty and dying and mystery. It is as if the world were a series of questions, and astonishment were the answer. A raindrop beads into perfection for a few seconds and collapses from the weight of its form.

Grand Manan

Nature speaks as though it were a lover.

—Octavio Paz

Another summer is warming the waters of the Bay of Fundy, with its rips and eddies, its extreme tides, its creatures of sea and air returning from global voyages. Once again I make my crossing to the island, sit at my window and watch what has changed and what has stayed the same. And when the sun breaks a week of rain and fog, I set out for water so I can get closer to the essence of the place, how its life is encompassed by what goes on offshore.

When the swells begin to rise in the deep channel, the water feels like a living body, our vessel a mote adrift in its cytoplasm. The rhythmic sway of tides measures the pull of planet and moon. I can't feel those forces in my body, though they must be there, made as I am from so much cellbound water. The human body is a poor instrument for sensing patterns of movement that guide the migration of whales, terns, butterflies, and geese. I cannot read with my body the earth's magnetic forces, the tracks of sun, stars, and ocean currents. What pushes or pulls the arctic tern forward when it migrates from its summer home in Iceland to its winter home in the Antarctic Ocean? Ways of knowing that a human body will never know. But the human body is a good instrument for making language, and that tool is the best means we've got for finding our way.

We ride the peaks and troughs of a long roll, heading out toward the Bulkhead where underwater tidal currents collide to produce an upwelling of organisms that make good feeding for sea mammals. Our ship is the schooner D'Sonoqua, designed and built by skipper James Bates when he lived in British Columbia. He named the ship after the Kwakiutl "Wild Woman of the Woods," the mythic creature who felt driven by civilization to live in the backwoods where she survives on what's at hand, makes what she needs when she needs it—a bed, a basket, a shawl—and leaves it behind when she's done. She embodies the wildness that survives technological progress, a good companion for the kind of man who can imagine himself neolithic, who never looks quite at home indoors, and whose contract with community seems always about to be dissolved by his affection for the sea. For a decade, since sailing the D'Sonoqua from Pacific to Atlantic Canada, James has skippered summer whale-watch tours out of Grand Manan in collaboration with a local cetacean research station. In winters he sails like a tern down the coast to more temperate shores. The roll is caused, he tells me, by the tide rushing at us as it debouches from the long narrow bay separating Nova Scotia from the main body of the continent. I jot this information in my pocket notebook.

"Are you part of the crew?" asks one of the tourists,

watching me juggle binoculars, notebook, and pen—field tools of the trade. "You look very official."

"No, no, just taking notes," I assure, casting off the burden of authority, though I do love letting the tourists know I'm a regular here, not a one-timer, not because it makes me more knowledgeable, but because it attests to my love for the place. My fellow travelers on this run are members of an Elder Hostel tour, all bundled brightly in polar fleece and Gortex, shoulders strung with cameras and video recorders, and guided by our shipboard naturalist, Laurie Murison, who studies the right whales making their annual migration to these waters and their calves making a first-time appearance.

I have no clear goal in mind for the notes I take, other than to help myself remember the intensities of the day, the mix of sensation and thought as it rises and falls with the swells. It's possible that in the notes some form will announce itself, and that they will lead to a poem or essay. It's possible they will not. But taking them forces a kind of attention that makes the experience richer, and attention is central to both artistic and spiritual practice.

We mingle with twelve finbacks, sleek and graceful whales, that glide up to the surface, blow, then slice back under. Storm petrels scoot across the water's surface like hydroplanes. A fish dragger passes, net stretched astern combing the water, where it will labor for hours, pulling in everything in its path. Fish stocks are depleted in the North Atlantic, and the government has set quotas, but fishermen complain that quotas don't work. Whatever's in the net gets scooped on deck. By the time the crew has sorted the legal from the illegal catch, most of the fish thrown back are already dead. Herring gulls, blackbacks, and fish gulls follow the dragger in a feeding party.

As we near the Bulkhead, tall plumed blows of finbacks gust into the air, the black skin gleaming for a moment in the sunlight before the surface lies blank. Each breath sounds like an explosion, and it is, Laurie explains. A finback exhalation jets out eleven hundred liters of air moving at four hundred miles per hour, the blast detonating as the whale breaches the surface, then misting off into silence as the whale goes under. We watch four or six feeding in a pod, then three or four pods. It's hard to keep track in the chaos of blows and dives. Three come along the port side, holding with our pace, close enough for us to see the white lip patch on the right side of their heads. It's one of few asymmetrical patterns in nature. Seen through the water, the patch gives off gradations of color, ripples of pale turquoise iridescence. Big orange colonies of phytoplankton have streaked the heads. As the whales glide beside our schooner, each training a huge watery eye on our boat, we all press against the starboard gunwale, exclaiming and gasping with joy, then race to the port side to catch the next fleeting spectacle. The camera and video enthusiasts jostle into one another and curse amiably as they ruin each other's shots or a camera automatically rewinds just at the moment a perfect shot is framed. Human squeals, groans, sighs, mechanical whirs, and the heavy gusting of whale breath—it's a fugue we're all playing, though it feels more like it's playing us. And then it stops. The surface goes glassy and quiet, and we settle down with tea and ginger-snaps, everyone smiling with satisfaction.

No one's prepared for the slow growl that rises off the water, the sound I feel enter my body by trembling straight through my chest rather than slipping into my ears. There's a finback lying surfaced beside us. Then a second finback emerges, letting out the same cavernous rumble. In seventeen years of field-work, Laurie has rarely heard such vocalizations, and she is as thrilled as a woman can be who is utterly sobered by her attention to detail. She notes the time, longitude, and latitude, then fills us in. The finback voice is among the loudest and deepest in the ocean, creating such long frequency waves that the animals easily can communicate forty miles across the bay, even one hundred miles across the Gulf of Maine. It's possible that if located in the right spot, they can talk underwater across ocean basins all the way from New England to Europe. But rarely do people hear finbacks vocalizing into the air. The behavior probably has nothing to do with our presence, announcing instead some urgency of breeding or appetite, the desires inspiring so much of the planet's song.

The sea to the north lies blank ahead of us as we bob along. Scanning the seam between sea and sky, I spot the first small white V of a right whale blow gusting up in the distance. We'd nearly forgotten, so many towering finback geysers, that this was the species *(Eubalaena glacialis)* we sought, the rarest of the large whales with only a few hundred left in the North Atlantic. They were driven nearly to extinction in the past century, because they were the "right whale" to hunt, more richly blubbered than other species and prone to float, living or dead, making them coveted prey. They have been protected from hunting for the past sixty years and now are worth more on the eastern U.S. seaboard as tourist attractions than as kill. Captain James powers the D'Sonoqua towards the V, and we approach in time to see a slow flukes-up dive, Laurie quickly snapping a photo of the animal's tail. From the details of shape, color, wounds, and scarring, she can identify individuals—three hundred fifty now listed in a catalog and monitored when they gather here with their calves to feed in midsummer. She's not sure what this year will hold, since censusing in the Caribbean during the past winter did not go well. The productivity of field research is as prone to seasonal fluctuations as are cetacean birth rates. In one of her best seasons, she saw one hundred right whales all at once and didn't know where to look first. But her most thrilling day, she says, was one of high seas, the boat crashing up and down through troughs, when she looked up into a wall of water to see a finback riding the swell above her.

Two more right whales lounge at the surface off our bow, one turning on its side and flippering as it passes. Two more dawdle off the stern. It's odd to see them lazing, fat and docile, in no hurry for the next dive. If finbacks are the greyhounds of cetaceans, then right whales are the mastiffs. Now another of these lumpen loungers, the biggest we've seen (maybe fifty feet long) breaks through the surface, mud smeared all over its massive head. No one knows what it means, but researchers have seen this before. They've lowered video cameras one hundred feet down and watched the whales scraping their foreheads on the sea floor. They may be feeding or scratching infestations of lice off their heads or who knows what. All the more pleasure for me that we don't know. Human beings behave as if nature were their sovereignty. When encountering something in nature we don't understand, suddenly we recognize that nature is sovereign not to us but to itself.

The tide slackens and the swells lay down flat. In the barely perceptible distance, a chaos of whale blows hatches the horizon, dozens of towering white fountains. So much energy is being expended that from a distance the disruption looks vaguely industrial. Then, trying to fix the image in my mind, I write in my notebook, "looks like a scene from a war movie." The simile seems so right and yet it's alarming how easily it comes to me, how estranged of the sea's daily business I am that an image of war seems easier to visualize than bursts of cetacean breath erupting randomly and rapturously into the air as the great mammals feast their way through the bay. And overhead a constant broken line of contrails marks the path of jets, each turning gracefully at the same unmarked spot in the air, arcing down from the pole as it heads toward Boston or New York City or Washington, D.C., in a sadly beautiful techno-ballet staged against the brilliant blue sky.

My family began visiting Grand Manan Island in 1954 when I was eight years old, and I have continued to do so every summer as an adult. It is the one place with which I have a continuous, if intermittent, relationship from childhood to the present—a place that has served as a relative constant in a time of rapid change, a place isolated enough that the elemental relationship between nature and culture has not been obscured by commercial development, a place where nature's intensities shape the life of body and soul. When I look for the underpinnings of my writing about the natural world, I find first this geographic footing. I suppose if I had spent every summer since childhood in Paris, my subject matter might be very different. But that is not the case, and I am grateful because at this point in history to know a place where a way of life is still shaped by nature's terms is to know something archetypally human, yet something that is leaking away from most people's lives. "The great poet," said T. S. Eliot, "in writing himself, writes his time." I have taken the statement to mean that the task of poetry—literature in general—is to understand what it means to live at *this* time in history as opposed to any other. And surely one of the defining characteristics of our time is the bleeding from the world of nature's complexity and of cultures shaped by nature's local terms.

The island is a true community, one shaped for the past two hundred years by small-scale commercial fishing. Islanders answer first to the sea, and they know human power always remains secondary to that of nature, a knowledge that makes them skeptical of just about any plan the government comes up with for the island's future. It is not that the community is self-contained. International relations have always figured in the island's thriving. They have sold salt pollack and cod to Chile, kippered herring to Great Britain, sardines and seaweed to the United States, and sea urchin eggs to Japan. Economic well-being is not, however, the private business of each separate family, but a public concern tied to shepherding marine resources. The commonwealth of the island depends upon the commonwealth of the sea. And those who work these treacherous waters know what it is to be humbled by the forces of nature. Every family on the island has lost loved ones to the sea, and they have nurtured a faith in powers beyond the human in order to cope with these losses. Talk of community in urban places—cultures that have become so economically complex that they have lost their tangible relationship with the terms nature sets for the place—always pales beside the reality of community on the island. I do not think community—a shared sense of purpose and belonging—is possible without a shared sense of reliance on local resources.

I have no sense of community in my urban life, beyond what I nurture in my professional life. And rich though it may be, this sense of community seems shallow compared to that on the island, where people know they owe their lives to nature and the greater forces of the universe, and they know how to express gratitude to these forces.

Stories help to hold the community together, a bond forming among those who have heard a story—the special society of those in the know, each of whom has had a chance to add two cents worth to the tale. The best stories celebrate how heroism and faith can visit ordinary lives. One my father told for years honored two fishermen lost at sea in a gale, stranded in their dory for days in high seas with no water, food, or compass, nothing but prayer for comfort. Asked later how he had survived the ordeal, one of the men replied quietly that they had been saved by "the third man in the boat." He meant Jesus, of course, and whether he had been a believer before or remained one after I do not know. The story reaffirmed an elemental cultural value that no one wanted to forget—the man was a hero not through deeds but through faith.

Last summer I heard a story that I suspect will serve as a vessel for a shift in cultural meaning. Some historical context will explain why the story spread so energetically throughout the island's five villages. For two hundred years Grand Mananers—a relatively stable population of twenty-five hundred—have earned a living fishing for herring, scallops, pollack, haddock, and lobsters. But the fishery in the North Atlantic has been drastically depleted by overfishing. The decline in the Bay of Fundy has not reached the extremes it has in Newfoundland, where the government closed most of the fisheries in the early 1990s, sentencing the fishermen and their families to unemployment compensation and cultural drift.

The most unique fishery on Grand Manan is the brush weir built to catch herring. The materials are simple—conifer stakes driven into shallow waters, topped with birch poles and laced with netted twine that forms a heart-shaped enclosure, the opening large enough for a seiner and dory to pull inside. The weir works by channeling schools of herring chased shoreward by larger groundfish into the enclosure. The skills for building and working the weirs have been handed down and refined from father to son for many generations. (Rarely do women work in the fishery on Grand Manan, unlike in Alaska, where women commonly work as skipper or crew.) Each weir is named—the Jubilee, the Corabell, the Mystery, the Intruder—and each weir is owned in shares like the old whaling vessels, so that its owners gain or lose together based on the catch. The device works because the Bay of Fundy has extreme tidal variations, making it possible for men to construct the weir at low tide, trap schools of herring at high tide, and seine out the weir when the water slackens to midtide. But harvesting out a weir is tricky business. If there are bountiful fish at a time when the market is poor, seining is useless. Waiting for market conditions (generally the sardine factory on the mainland) to improve may mean the herring will escape.

The successful weir fisherman has an array of skills broader than the most capable urban business-man. He is construction engineer, onboard naviga-tor and mechanic, marine naturalist, ichthyologist, weatherman, market analyst, environmental resource manager, and supervisor of a cross-generational group of workers who bring specialized skills into all stages of the enterprise. The skill I most revere for its sim-plicity and refinement is that of feeling for herring. To gauge how many fish are trapped in the weir, a man rows a dory into the weir and drops a weighted line into the water. From the feel of herring that bump into the line, he can say how many hogsheads of fish are schooling below and when it's time for seining. Such a man is nearly as native to these wa-ters as herring, rockweed, and whales.

But the future of weir fishing on the island is in question as native stocks decline and more highly in-dustrialized fisheries are introduced. Salmon-farming pens appear to be the most economically promising new industry on the island. These operations are generally capitalized by mainland or overseas com-panies, and they employ workers in routine tasks—feeding manufactured fishmeal to penned smolts—for which the workers are paid an hourly wage and hold no share in ownership. The salmon pens are built of plastic tubing manufactured who knows where and as-sembled by plastic welders brought in from the main-land. There is nothing homegrown in the materials or methods, no promise of shared wealth in a bountiful year nor shared hardship in a lean one. There is no stake placed on the well-being of marine habitat, because aquaculture operations construct an artificial habitat. There is little job satisfaction and none of the generations-old pride that the weir fishery engendered; there is only the thin security of a regular wage.

Tourism is the other signpost for the island's economic future. There is some hope that small-scale, nature-based travel will help the island's economy, but it is difficult to imagine that a man who once built a weir, felt for herring with his bare hands, and navigated the perilous rips of the bay would take much satisfaction from being a campground handyman or bed-and-breakfast clerk.

Into the waters of these insecurities about the economic future sailed the story of Wayne Ingalls rescuing two right whales. My mother heard it while playing tennis with the round-robin group that meets in North Head on sunny summer mornings. She and I spend a few summer weeks together on the island now that my father has passed on and I have drifted into a prolonged period of being single. It's a fellowship we treasure, though it's not without the tensions that most families suffer. She's proud that in her late eighties the island affords her an active social life—tennis, bridge, tea, and calling on old friends. It's a hedge for her against the fear she'll become dependent as she ages. I'm as intent as she is at proving that I can live richly alone, working monkishly at the desk all day or wandering far into the bird-loud woods. Though each of us feels an intimate absence in our life that the other can't fill, the island is a bridge that joins us. We fall in love with it in our separate ways summer after summer—arriving to think that it's too simple and modest to engender the enthusiasms we've felt for it in past years, then after a few days of picking up rocks on the beach, chatting with neighbors, eating locally grown greens, berries, and fish, watching the tides rise and fall, we slide again into harmony with the place and with each other. And we share our fears that the place will change under economic pressure, will lose its simplicity, beauty, and integrity, meaning we will lose the annual replenishing of those qualities in our souls.

She breezed into the house with the news.

"Well, *we* have a local hero," she boasted. A possession of great measure clearly had come our way.

It was June, early in the herring season. A lot of money had gone into building weirs and nothing yet had come out of them, when our neighbor found two right whales trapped inside his weir. Fish and sea mammals find it easy to get into the structure, but difficult to get out. The gate points shoreward. Instinct tells the animals that freedom lies seaward. Once inside the enclosure, they swim around in confused circles. This is fine for herring, but when a whale gets stuck in a weir loaded with herring it will eat its fill, then tear the nets to get loose. As traditional in the region as brush weirs is the slaughtering of predators that invade the nets. It is not unusual to hear rifle blasts echoing over the water as a fisherman dispatches seals robbing a family of its livelihood. In recent years, however, new relationships have been developing, thanks in part to the work of cetacean researchers, and in part to changing values among fishermen about sharing the livelihood of the sea.

The story of the release spread like brushfire. Researchers had brought in the predator net and the whales were set free, along with sixty thousand dollars worth of herring, the first catch of the year. It was that sacrifice which made the act heroic. A lot of people are no longer sure what it takes to be a hero these days, so many icons having fallen. Even the venerable occupation of working the sea has been called into question by the excesses that have impoverished marine habitats. The story mattered to people because their pride in it told them that in spite of economic peril, something mattered to them more than money. That a man would sacrifice his livelihood to save two endangered whales said that those other lives were sacred. A lot of people are also no longer sure what it takes for a thing to be sacred. Separate from any specific religious connotation, I take it to mean deserving respect and protection. When a thing is sacred, it is protected from violation; it inspires ethical obligation and sacrifice.

Stories are the way we tell each other who we are, the way we cross the borders that separate us. They are so much a part of our ordinary discourse that we hardly notice them. We make a new acquaintance and ask,

Where are you from? How did you come to live here? We run into a friend and ask, What have you been up to? We come home at night to loved ones and ask, How was your day? And if one takes the time to really answer the question, a story unfolds. Do you want to hear the *whole* story? we ask hopefully, because we know that the other person will come to know us if we tell the story, for example, of being born in Park City to Mormon parents who wanted to be ranchers but ended up being suburbanites, and how we had to leave to become ourselves because there was no longer a futuristic dream of inhabiting the land and living off its fat but one of navigating the city and its dynamic contradictions until we got to that new place and then hungered for the land we'd left behind. The story, not information, is what we inhabit.

When the beliefs and values of a society are breaking down, stories help people to see what is going on, to uncover a new pattern or truth, to compensate in the inner life for chaos in the outer life. To "story," now an obsolete verb, meant to narrate in painting, sculpture, or song. Some stories shape who we are collectively as a family, region, nation, or civilization. There are master stories—the Garden of Eden and Manifest Destiny—that become a resource underlying a culture like a gigantic aquifer on which everyone draws. I am particularly fond of the way William Kittredge has written about the politics of storytelling.

> We figure and find stories, which can be thought
> of as maps or paradigms in which we see our
> purposes defined; then the world drifts and our
> maps don't work any more, our paradigms and
> stories fail, and we have to reinvent our under-
> standings, and our reasons for doing things. . . .
> That's what stories are for, to help us see for
> ourselves as we go about the continual business
> of reimagining ourselves.

He cautions against ignoring the changing world and sticking to some story too long. If we do so "we are likely to find ourselves in a great wreck," such as we find all around us in the collapse of natural systems. We live in the closing chapter of a story five hundred years old. It began with the voyages of discovery, which taught our ancestors that the world was much larger than they thought it was, that they could leave home and find a better place to start over. And it is ending with the world feeling much smaller and more vulnerable than we thought, the mistakes of our ancestors and everyone else's, burdens we're stuck with because there is no place free of history left for us to go.

The story ends in our lifetimes as the last indige-nous people leave their primary relationship with nature and join the abstracted world of commercial enterprise. We no longer each go to forest, field, and sea for sustenance, though our dependence upon them is no less real; we go to store, catalog, and mall, money the crop we spend ourselves to cultivate. We are less materially connected with nature than our ancestors, their hands in the dirt and blood of living, and the consequence is that we are less spiritually connected with nature. Being less spiritually connected to nature, we feel little prohibition against violating it. One reason for the current interest in and importance of nature writing is that it leads us back, at least imaginatively, to experiencing intimacy with the natural world.

Sometimes—dark times—the most optimistic story I can muster of the human future is that our descendants will leave Earth to colonize other planets, mining from lifeless soils the elements with which to synthesize the chemicals they need to survive. Gone will be the rich aesthetic beauty of entangled rain forest and sinuous river, the lemur and leopard, damselfly and blue morhpo, water lily and pampas grass, sugar maple and banyan. Gone will be the lessons of seasonal and generational decline and renewal, the complexity so marvelous it is at once one unified thing and countless differentiated things. Human beings will rise to the challenge of creating natural museums to teach about our biological and planetary past. But these will be thin and spiritless experiences compared to the thickness of riding a dugout canoe into the Amazon jungle, a dozen golden spider monkeys swinging tree to tree in your path and stopping to watch you watch them, the caiman and boutu swimming under your hull and making it tremble.

The most ardent futurists speak of extraterrestrial colonization as inevitable and urgent. Earth, they say, will be smacked by an asteroid, depleted of resources, or subsumed in the sun's engulfing death spasm. If human life is to continue, we will have to leave our homeland, and there is so very much to learn—generations worth—before we will be capable of the leap, that we had better work now toward that goal. Maybe this is the way organisms are—using up what they've got and looking for more elsewhere. Some destruction is required to live. We cannot eat rocks and air. Yet why should one organism eat so greedily that all others are imperiled? It is a problem of measure. When we're finished grazing in the garden, I want there to be some garden left. This is more than an aesthetic desire—though surely it is the beautiful complexity of nature that woos me. It is a moral desire. To use nature beyond its capacity to restore itself is to destroy the force and process that have given us our lives. We have not fallen from nature, we have risen from it; all human accomplishment, feeling, and belief along with flesh and blood are rooted in that generative power. Even our strange human inwardness that imagines such guiding abstractions as faith, justice, love, and compassion is a gift of nature. The theory of evolution, our long genetic entanglement with all the other living things, is not at odds with theories of the sacred. It locates the sacred in living things. I believe we owe nature the deep sense of gratitude that people once expressed to their gods. The earth's life is finite, as is my own, and these are realities I accept with sorrow, the place and the passage made sacred by their limits.

A few days after my right whale excursion, I make an outing to Wood Island with Canadian cultural geographer Joan Marshall. We've become good friends during the past decade while she has been working on Grand Manan to understand how cultural changes are altering the landscape. We both fear that a new market paradigm rushing onto the island in the wake of depleted resources will overwhelm its traditional values—the sense of community based on environmental sustainability and personal integrity based on the superiority of local knowledge. She has noted the increasingly industrialized appearance of beaches since salmon farming came to the island, in contrast to the quaint and homey shingled smokehouses of the past. Thirty years ago there were two hundred working smokehouses on the island; in 1998 there was one. Even Seal Cove Beach, the prettiest big white sand beach on the island, now sports huge black snakes of plastic tubing awaiting fabrication into fish cages. We try not to get each other too depressed about the changes. After all, we say, as outsiders what can we do? We agree that our role can be to show what's happening as best we see it, to bring stories from other places to bear upon the unfolding story of this place, and to communicate what is valuable to us as respectful outsiders about this place—what aspects of local culture and nature seem most deserving of respect and preservation. But our outing this day is a simpler pleasure.

Wood Island is a small bump on the map off-shore from the Grand Manan village of Seal Cove.

Early in the 1900s it was a thriving community with its own weirs, smokehouses for curing herring, post office, church, and general store. The 1948 map hanging in my living room shows thirty houses dotting the islet's surface. Today no one lives there, except in the summer when two guys from Nova Scotia come to stay in an old family place while they putter back and forth to Grand Manan doing carpenter work. It also harbors one surly part-time hermit who, when he's not in Seal Cove, lives in a hovel cobbled into an old house foundation. My neighbor tells me that when some school kids came out on a class trip, he threatened to skin them alive if they ever snooped around his place again. Once a year the Wood Island Reformed Baptist Church, built in 1922, holds a reunion in the sanctuary, followed by a baptism at the breakwater in Seal Cove. Island baptisms are no tepid affair. Usually they entail a bone-chilling full immersion in the icy waters of the bay. My mother once watched a woman dressed in her Sunday best endure the ritual. Two men wearing suits waded her out knee deep, then leaned her backward down into the frigid water. Three times they dipped her, and from my mother's telling she did look like she had the fear of God in her when she emerged.

Rodger Maker ferries us over in his wooden runabout, crunching onto the gravel beach and leaving us to meander for the day. We hike past the Quonset house of the carpenters—rough-hewn flagpole painted white and strung with new nylon line, pea patch, hummingbird feeder, woodpile neatly stacked and covered with old plywood, purple martin house on pole, sawhorse, zigzagged rows of black plastic pipe on the roof for hot water, horseshoe pits—a tidy masculine domesticity. We hike up the grassy lane to the cemetery, and finding it freshly mowed we walk among the half grassed-over stones. A small marker—maybe ten inches by eight—of grainy limestone is framed with two bouquets of plastic flowers stuck in the ground. An even smaller stone marbled with yellow lichen bears the name "Faith R." cut into its narrow top and on the vertical face the inscription, "Budded on Earth to Bloom in Heaven." Only twenty or so stones remain standing in the cemetery. Some are real headstones—boulders cut from the field and set on edge. But mostly the cemetery is an empty grassy field, most of the gravestones long ago fallen and subsumed by the sod. Many of the remaining stones mark the passing of children who lived only a few months; many are decorated with silk, plastic, or Kleenex bouquets. The grave of Wilbert C. Tidd, March 14, 1937–July 6, 1937, is graced with a sleeping limestone lamb and a willow garland, freshly made, held together with baggy ties and laced with silk leaves and flowers. More than sixty years ago a person died after living fewer than four months, and he is still remembered with handmade gifts here in the middle of nowhere where not a soul lives the year round.

We hike up the grassy lane to the church and find it unlocked, the old wooden pews arcing from a central partition so that they look like the skeleton of a great fish. On each sill of the twelve arched windows stands a blue glass water bottle ("Feralito Vuliaggo & Sons—Twenty Ounce" written in raised glass script on each one). The floor is covered with a sheet of linoleum printed with a pattern made to look like a rug. An old wooden pendulum clock hangs on the wall, ticking in the empty sanctuary with ferocious insistence.

"You can't escape it," Joan says.

"A sound surely invoked in many sermons," I reply.

I play the old pump organ on which only one pedal works, hymnal open to "The Sheltering Rock." "O why will ye die . . ." the hymn beseeches as if faith gave one a choice in the matter. On the lectern sits the huge aged Bible, tarnished metal clasps holding closed its embossed leather cover, a white doily stitched with chalice and cross draped beneath it. The pages are wrinkled from decades of fog, a few tattered ones hanging loose. A poem is etched on a stained glass window:

Fundy tides run deep
then ebb away.
From across the waters
men and women came
to settle here
like so many generations
that come and go.
And now their children
and children's children
scattered all across the lands.

We hike farther along the grass lane into a forest of collapsing houses, gray lath boards splintering like brittle bones, roofs concave, walls buckling, the structures gently leaning, taking decades to yield, gray shingles splaying and feathering, slowly the houses going back into the earth, letting go of the human insistence on right angles, easing back to the soft roundness of Earth. Enormous banks of white and pink tea roses run wild and billowy over the ruin, their fragrance making us swoon. And rising there among the falling houses is a chorus of bird-song so dense as to sound purely orchestral—liquid piping and bubbling, percussive twittering and saw-ing, one screech, then a series of caws. One bird holds its note while vibrating it, another flits ran-domly up and down the scale, and another rings and rings its one-note alarm.

"I thought it was a cell phone," I confess sheep-ishly to Joan.

"I thought a doorbell," she replies.

Joan knows a few birds by their songs. The winter wren or redstart, she thinks, makes the complex song—not repeated elements, but random ones. Red crossbills chatter high in the spruces. The wood thrush makes the melodic song with the emphatic conclusion. And the black-throated green warbler chants *z-z-z-z-zoo-zee*.

We find a forest of twinflowers *(Linnaea borealis)*, the plant so esteemed by Linnaeus that he gave it his name and had his portrait painted among them. Five petals form a small bell, dark pink inside, white fringed, blooms paired on a round red stem, leaf elliptic with shallow teeth on the edges, a creeping plant that forms a blanket of twinned, nodding bells. We find the pink-striped flowers of common wood sorrel, wondering why it shares a name and apparently little else with the red-tasseled sheep sorrel that we've both picked wild for salads. We hike through the gull rookery at the island's southern end, carrying sticks over our heads for protection against the chaos of gulls flying over their nests. There are no young in sight, but the place is hyperactive with calls and flybys, the ground a hummocky mix of peat, yellowed grass, matted rounds of abandoned nests with bird droppings all clayed together. Here and there a swampy seep breaks loose with an outcry of wild iris blooms. Little white tufts of gull down flitter by on the breeze. When we arrive at the island's backside, we spot a kingfisher locked in muscular hover over the water, and we lock ourselves in place to wait for its dive. Then we bushwhack along the shore, trail long gone from this wilder reach, billygoating up ledges and down to the stony beach, through scraggly stands of spruce and across spans of bald rock. We come upon a geologic meeting point on the beach. My best guess as to the rock types—red slate interbedded with red conglomerate abutting green and quartz-laced serpentine. We wish a geologist had tagged along to tell us the story of the rocks' formation.

I love Joan's companionship. I cannot think of many women friends who would take such delight in being lost in a small woods with nothing to entertain us but the pleasure of birdcalls and our own curiosity. We speculate about the rise and fall of the Wood Island culture, a local lifeway that worked for a few generations and then stopped working. As much pleasure as we take in seeing the place fall out of human hands and back into nature, we wish we knew more about why and how the community flourished here in its heyday. We imagine for the island a small historical reconstruction of village, smoke sheds, and weirs—oral histories on tape so that what was learned goes forward. But natural history has its own way of recording what has happened. The exuberance of birdsong uninhibited by village life, the roses unpruned engulfing foundations, the rookery gulls certain in their territorial supremacy—these are the real living history museum, the end of one way of life giving rise to others. It is the pattern in nature that gives deepest solace—ripeness may fall into decay and disorder, but decay and disorder fall, in turn, back into ripeness.

We hike on, following the wooded shoreline north, scouting for a path that will bring us back to where we started. Suddenly as we elbow through a thick stand of spruce trees, a space on the edge of denser woods fills with an indistinct shape. Tense, timid, gentle, alive, it slips away leaving ferns to wave in the wake of its passing. I stand frozen, staring at the fronds until they are still. I look up to see Joan, bright with energy, staring at the same spot of green.

"Did you see that?" she asks.

"I think so," I reply. And we try to figure out what we have almost seen. Joan thinks something furry, big, blocky—a little bear. We laugh at how impossible that is. I think something fat, round, fuzzy, slow as a cow. We laugh again.

"No, not slow," Joan adds. "It disappeared so quickly. Gentle."

"Yes," I agree. "A sheep?"

We recall that off-islands like this one often have been used as fenceless pastures. On nearby Long Island a few sheep run wild, keeping the shrubbery nice and trim all winter for when the summer residents return. No, we agree, we would have seen wool pulled off on the rose bushes by now. We'll never know what we didn't see, but having almost seen it together makes us certain some feral presence watched our passing for as long as it dared, then when it saw our attention moving its way, made itself scarce. For those tense moments, we felt it take the measure of us, and we took its measure, our bodies startled awake by another's living energy—Panic, as the ancients called it, filled with the sacred *furor*.

We find our way, of course, keeping the ocean to our right and the woods to our left, until we rise up a steep ledge and land in a huge rhubarb patch sprawling into a meadow tall with timothy.

"Civilization!" I exclaim and pull loose the red, fruity stalks to stuff them in my daypack.

A shingled cottage, boarded shut, stands on the edge of the meadow, a boat winch rusted useless stands on the edge of the beach, and beyond them a grassy lane leads through the woods—the shortcut back to where we will meet the boat to go home. We cut west, gnarly wild rose bushes spilling along the borders of the forest, and the forest spilling over with song. There lying on the matted grass in front of my hiking boot is a little tuft of wool. We laugh in pleasure that our speculations appear redeemed. We've been scouted by the last of a remnant tribe of sheep. I pick up the tuft and sniff the lanolin and wild rose smells, still fresh in the fibers. I slip the tuft in my pocket, knowing that one whiff will take me back here when I'm home and lonely.

> When we were born, we were torn from wholeness; in love we have all felt ourselves returning to the original wholeness. That is why poetic images transform the beloved into nature—a mountain, water, a cloud, a star, a wood, the sea, a wave—and why in turn nature speaks as though it were a lover.
>
> —Octavio Paz

A small footnote to our adventure: the day after our hike, Joan is still curious about our encounter with the elusive animal. She calls me to say she asked Rodger, who had ferried us to the island, if there were any feral sheep on Wood Island. He said there might still be and he told her a story. One winter day from the breakwater in Seal Cove he had seen a sheep out there stranded on a ledge at low tide. At high tide he took his skiff over and in the cold battering of wind and waves he wrangled the animal into his boat and returned it to safety on the island. The next day, he looked out again across the water and there was the sheep stranded on the same ledge. Forget it, he said to himself, and went about his chores. Later that spring he found the carcass washed into a gully on shore near the ledge. The only sense he could make of this was that he thought the sheep had gone out there to die. And this seemed wonderful to all of us, this kind of knowing that moves a body where it needs to go, human intelligence, in all its marvelous inventiveness and compassion, humbled before that of a wasted wild sheep.

Provincetown

Amidst the downward tendency and proneness of things, when every voice is raised for a new road or another statute, or a subscription of stock, for an improvement in dress, or in dentistry, for a new house or a larger business, for a political party, or the division of an estate,—will you not tolerate one or two solitary voices in the land, speaking for thoughts and principles not marketable or perishable? Soon these improvements and mechanical inventions will be superseded; these modes of living lost out of memory; these cities rotted, ruined by war, by new inventions, by new seats of trade, or the geologic changes: all gone, like the shells which sprinkle the seabeach with a white colony to-day, forever renewed to be forever destroyed. But the thoughts which these few hermits strove to proclaim by silence, as well as by speech, not only by what they did, but by what they forbore to do, shall abide in beauty and strength, to reorganize themselves in nature, to invest themselves anew in other, perhaps higher endowed and happier mixed clay than ours, in fuller union with the surrounding system.

—Ralph Waldo Emerson

On a bright summer's day I sit in the upstairs reading room of the Provincetown Public Library copying Emerson's words into my notebook. *"Nature,"* I write, "in the common sense, refers to essences unchanged by man." Other visitors sit at the long oak table in the crowded room doing crossword puzzles, reading the *New Yorker,* browsing the mysteries—a roomful of misfits to the commerce that drives this town somewhere it doesn't really want to go. I've done my time on Commercial Street, of course, so I don't claim any transcendence over the hunger to shop and gawk. But on this day, the bustle repels me, and I need nothing so much as the quiet company of readers and thinkers.

I came to town for the art-monastic life—what's necessary and nothing more—one room where the bed serves as couch, the table serves as desk, and the daily meditation is a walk from Brewster Street in the east end to the breakwater at the west end of town. I came here to focus under the scrutiny of sunlight intensified by the cape's extremity, a spindle of sand stretching sixty miles out into the sea, the light jacked up by water and sand and lack of urban distractions. I came here to write this essay—a simple task, I thought, to articulate the aesthetic and philosophic underpinnings of my work.

"The currents of the Universal Being circulate through me." I copy more words into my notebook, I close the book, set it on the table, and walk out into the vacationing throng, marveling at the colors of human business—brand new this year: dusty rose, lichen green, sandy beige, and cloud gray—so much invention all aimed at getting me to buy. At Marine Specialties I elbow down dim, chaotic aisles lined with bins of salvaged seashells, distressed T-shirts, brass bullet casings, and secondhand restaurant linens, and because it is gray outside I try on an Army surplus khaki raincoat that smells of sour mold. I like what the funky style makes of me, but fear that no amount of sunshine will heal the fabric of its stench. I walk next door—a trendy Boston clothing company—and try on overpriced sweaters and buy the midnight blue chenille cardigan because it makes me feel beautiful, its blue nothing really like midnight, more like the dark watery hue of Earth as seen from the moon.

All of this—the walk, the reading, the notes, the browsing and buying—is distraction from the task at hand. But every writer knows that distraction is how to find the subject—no point running up to it head on, because that will only scare it away, that skittish animal of what one intends. Artists live by their contradictions. Write what I believe about writing? If I knew what I believed I would not need to write. The city of whatever I make will fall to ruin—"forever renewed to be forever destroyed"—so why is the hunger to say the inner life into form any more sacred than the hunger to shop and consume?

I walk on toward my studio, thinking of the mounting chaos of notes I will have to face when I return to my desk. Perishable, yes, all of it perishable. Unmarketable, yes (though I would be wise to keep this news from the esteemed publisher awaiting my words), because art is a way of giving to a world too full of human taking, and it is most authentic when it asks nothing back from the world than that it mix with the abounding clay. The storm clouds darken over me, closing me to my surroundings as I brood through the jostle of the street. At the stretch of town where I expect to run the gauntlet between over-eager menu hawkers stumping on the doorsteps of competing restaurants, I'm surprised to find conversations taking place, tourists and shills alike milling about in front of shops and cafés, the flow of commerce stanched by a weird and idle friendliness. I slow to meet the unexpected pace. It feels as if a sudden easy mutualism has replaced the predatory stalkings that crowd the street.

I am speaking metaphorically, of course. Such terms as commensalism, mutualism, and parasitism are meant to describe relationships between species. Commensalism is a relationship in which one species benefits from the association, while the other species in the partnership neither benefits nor suffers. Millipedes and silverfish, for example, live among army ants, scavenging on the refuse of their hosts without damaging them. Mutualism (or symbiosis) is the more utopian arrangement in which all parties benefit—the long-nosed bat nectars on saguaro cactus flowers, doing the sex work of the plant's reproduction; "the becoming-wasp of the orchid" meets "the becoming-orchid of the wasp," in the formulation of Deleuze and Guattari. A zoo of microbes thriving in the human gut helps us to thrive on the embarrassment of riches that is the human diet. Parasitism is the nastiest of the relationships, an organism so bent on glutting itself it will eat a host to death. Mutualism is my personal favorite—it doesn't ask too much, neither agony nor ecstasy, for either partner. They just get along without getting in one another's way, while mutual benefits accrue that neither partner intended.

Our species is so willfully adaptive that we seem able to employ any of these strategies if they serve our purposes. Our primary strategy has been as top predator, an animal that kills other animals to live but rarely finds itself prey. My brand new science encyclopedia tells me that "predators are usually bigger and more powerful than their prey, and their population is smaller—if the predator became more widespread than the prey, the population of the predator would inevitably fall." Any top predator, in other words, that works too efficiently will put itself out of business, unless it can think up a new business to replace the old.

Hunting mammoths and giant tree sloths worked for our ancestors for as long as those megafauna survived. A recent issue of the journal *Science* reports that the arrival of humans in any place has been bad news for large mammals for the past fifty thousand years. Human beings seem to start out in a place as predator and end as parasite, killing whatever sustains us. So far we have been clever enough to come up with new strategies when old ones fail: hunting takes a dive and we settle down on the farm to have our prey ready at hand; population rises, the farm begins to fail, we fight with our neighbors, then move to a new place and build a city as a fortress; population rises, the city dazzles us with its smartness and charm, and we forget we ever needed the earth, so enraptured we become with our inventions; population rises, the city begins to fail, we fight with our neighbors, then move back to the land finding earth, air, and water ruined by our neglect; there's nowhere left to go where we won't run into our failures, so we stay put and try to clean things up. Or maybe we just go shopping to try to make ourselves into something as new as the products on rack and shelf.

So, the power goes out in Provincetown, and a sudden easy mutualism breaks out on Commercial Street. The shops and restaurants lock their doors. People linger on the sidewalk, spill onto the street. Cars and trucks give up on progress, drivers leaning out their windows to chat with neighbors. There is nothing to gain or lose. The computers are down. The lighting is down. The griddles and ovens and microwaves are down. And the people are up, cheered by the futility of whatever had been their goals. What happened? everyone asks. How long will it last? Where can we go to eat? We all slow down to the pace of nowhere to go, and our lives look strange to us, and that wakes us up and makes us happy.

Then I see Marie Howe, who is also living at Brewster Street and trying to write, and I can see the cloud of her struggle still with her, though she too has left her studio to walk. Let's go eat, we agree, and find one place dimly lit with a generator and open for business. She too is working on a project that will not yield itself to her. She too has walked, she has made notes, she has read and read. She can feel the form of the new thing inside her, or she can feel the need that thing has to be in a form. But she has not yet been able to satisfy the need. Eliot was right: "In order to arrive at what you do not know / You must go by a way which is the way of ignorance." There is no ecstasy in that way. So why do we bother? But we know why. When we read

> and so each venture
> Is a new beginning, a raid on the inarticulate
> With shabby equipment always deteriorating
> In the general mess of imprecision of feeling . . .

we clap our hands to our hearts in gratitude that the unsayable has simply been said. Why? Some deep chord in us is struck when form is realized—a chord in which nature must always be one of the notes because to make art is to practice the form-making compulsion of nature, exercising "wild mind," to use Gary Snyder's term for how the enactment of consciousness mirrors that of nature. "'Wild' is a name for the way that phenomena continually actualize themselves"—here a saguaro, there a cypress; here a raven's *prruk,* there a warbler's *cheedle cheedle che che che che;* here a sonnet, there a free-forming cloud of a poem.

> music heard so deeply
> That it is not heard at all, but you are the music
> While the music lasts.

Art-making honors the life of the spirit by channeling incessant human desire toward self-revelation and connection with others, rather than toward obsessive consumption and controlling behavior over others. Why do we do it? I ask Marie, whose wisdom always comes from the heart. *It's our song.*

Of all the views I love in Provincetown, none holds its place in my mind more serenely than the crest on Route 6, from which a traveler gets the first glimpse of town. The land makes its last graceful gesture, winding into a sandy curl shaped by the ocean that surrounds it and sparkles on a good day like the skin of a bluefish. And the town rests in the curvature, gray shingled houses clustered like nestlings. That serenity, of course, is an illusion created by distance. No place of human habitation is secure or innocent or uncomplicated. Provincetown's fishing fleet is endangered by overfishing and upscale tourist development. The drinking water is in short supply and of questionable quality. The town has no more room for its garbage. Its historic status as an art colony is continually challenged by rabid commercialism—when the prices go up, the artists and writers must move out. And more loved men than anyone can bear to remember have died from a virus that wears a disguise of long-stemmed sugars enabling it to get through the body's usually masterful defenses. What comfort can there be in a view—the spiral of sand, the dazzling bay, the granite watchtower, and the huddle of skylit homes— when the beauty of life is always compromised by damage, suffering, and loss?

I've argued with another poet-friend about beauty.

He swears we no longer experience it, and that our poetry is an answer to that bleakness. But when he lived in Berkeley, he'd regularly escape the street-crazies and smog by driving north to Point Reyes—California's analogue to Cape Cod. He would not write about natural beauty, though he sought it for comfort, because he was convinced our language has been so tainted by history, politics, and advertising that a poem could no longer pretend to represent anything but itself. I argued that it was that very abrasion between the experience of beauty and what the culture sells us that makes us need to write, makes us fierce to enact our passion for the truth, makes us wild to reclaim the language from its abusers and polluters so that it conveys the wholeness of life's contradictions, celebrating beauty and lamenting its diminishment and loss.

If the spirit of a place has anything to do with what a poet makes, then it must be the intensity of light (two f-stops brighter than New York) and the extreme geography that so infuse the mind in Provincetown and make one more reflective. With all that jazzed-up light, the excitement of photons bouncing off water and sand, even the ordinary air says, *Notice me.* This energy makes the place artful for anyone who believes John Cage's maxim (roughly paraphrased here from my memory) that the function of art is to wake us up to the very life we are living. Those qualities of place have drawn generations of writers and artists to Provincetown—a shifting constellation including Eugene O'Neill and the Provincetown Players,

Hans Hoffman and the abstract expressionists, John Dos Passos, Norman Mailer, Mary Oliver, Alan Dugan, Stanley Kunitz, and the many many lights drawn to town by the Fine Arts Work Center, which Kunitz and Dugan and the beloved painter Myron Stout helped to found. I like to think that every artist who spends time working in such a place adds some element to the atmosphere that makes the air richer or creates a geomagnetic anomaly that makes it easier for another artist to come here, sit still, look at things, reflect, and figure out how to get what's enlivening onto the page or canvas, into the steel or clay.

Not that good work can't be done in Boston or the Bronx, hiking through the rainforest in Borneo or driving a tractor in Indiana. It simply helps, as in any act of dissent, to know that one is not alone. And writing poetry is an act of dissent in at least three ways: economically, because the poet labors to make a thing that will never be worth money; temporally, because the poem is an argument with the erosive passage of time; and politically, because in an age that values aggregate data, poetry—all true art—insists upon the passionate importance of the individual.

The turning inward to explore the world through the lens of subjective experience does not necessarily mean a turning away from the world. Denise Levertov turned Wordsworth's lament inside out by writing "the world is / not with us enough." Her poetics insisted upon both the lyric impulse—the song of the soul singing in the present moment—and the political impulse—the cry for social justice and peace. Her poetic spirit infuses mine, though trying to honor these two opposing impulses can cause a chronic psychic whiplash. Just when attention is focused on the inner excitement of consciousness, the world calls you a solipsist and demands your attention. Try to tell the world what you think of it, and consciousness will insist that *it*—consciousness itself—is the only thing you can know, and that you can only know it in its passing, so you had better take heed, *right now*. But Levertov found balance in the meditative mode, which asks for both introspection and realism—or as Muriel Rukeyser suggested, the meeting of consciousness and the world—and she wove a tenuous unity out of contradictions. I take that lesson to heart.

For me, the natural world in all its evolutionary splendor is a revelation of the divine—the inviolable matrix of cause and effect that reveals itself to us in what we *cannot* control or manipulate no matter how pervasive our meddling. This is the reason that our technological mastery over nature will always remain flawed. The matrix is more complex than our intelligence. We may control a part, but the whole body of nature must incorporate the change, and we are not capable of anticipating how it will do so. We will always be humbled before nature, even as we destroy it. And to diminish nature beyond its capacity to restore itself, as our culture seems perversely bent to do, is to desecrate the sacred force of Earth to which we owe a gentler hand. That the diminishment has been caused by abuses of human power make this issue political. Why should one species have the right to deprive so many others of their biological heritage and future? To write about nature, to record the magnificence, cruelty, and mysteriousness of it, is then an act both spiritual and political.

Italo Calvino describes how literature's interior explorations can be put to political use.

> Literature is necessary to politics above all when it gives a voice to whatever is without a voice, when it gives a name to what as yet has no name, especially to what the language of politics excludes or attempts to exclude. I mean aspects, situations, and languages both of the outer and of the inner world, the tendencies repressed both in individuals and in society. Literature is like an ear that can hear things beyond the understanding of the language of politics; it is like an eye that can see beyond the color spectrum perceived by politics. Simply because of the solitary individualism of his work, the writer may happen to explore areas that no one has explored before, within himself or outside, and to make discoveries that sooner or later turn out to be vital areas of collective awareness.

My early interests as a poet were to understand the modernist and postmodernist traditions, and to locate myself within their trajectory. And these traditions set aesthetic concerns in opposition to social ones—the artist as rebel, dissident, and iconoclast.

But the wellspring for that iconoclastic energy was for me the belief that art can be a voice of moral and spiritual empathy, an antidote to the coldhearted self-interest that drives so much of American culture.

> I have a hunger
> for harmony that I feed with dissent.

Realizing the importance of nature as a subject was a slow process of conversion for me. Way stations along the route: hearing Richard Nelson speak about writing his beautifully meditative book *The Island Within* after decades of working as a cultural anthropologist and his explaining that he had decided to write about what he loved; hearing Stanley Kunitz say to Fellows at the Work Center that originality in art could come only from what was unique in one's character and experience, not from manipulating the surface of one's technique; remembering that all of my life I have hungered for wild places and all of my life wild places have fed me and that this is central to who I am and would have to inform my aesthetic decisions; sitting up in bed alone as a child, darkness surrounding me, and staring at the mystery of how I came to exist in the world in this body, and how it is an impossible fact that I will one day stop being here; assessing what I most love about being here and what I most would like to understand and contribute before leaving; Grand Manan, that place as my teacher—how it is impossible to see nature and culture as opposed forces there, how the island has taught me that culture *is* nature in the form that is us.

I first came to Provincetown in 1984, the first of four years I lived and wrote here. The move came at a pivotal time—my daughter at prep school, my second marriage wearing thin after only two years, fifteen years of working in public health and living in the woods of northern Vermont feeding my determination to see what I could make of a life in writing. Raised in a culturally privileged family in Connecticut, I fell as a mother at eighteen into poverty, shame, and neglect. I learned two vital lessons from the hardship: self-reliance and an ethic of service to others. I worked, after the worst of it— welfare mother, dishwasher, waitress, farmhand, Linotype operator—as a paraprofessional counselor, then administrator, in family planning and sex education programs. The rewards were genuine—helping women make decisions for which I had had no help. But all along I was writing in seclusion, and there was a hollowness to my career. I felt that I was faking it at work, while my desire to be a writer was my real self.

Provincetown brought me into the culture of writing. It wasn't my first experience of such a culture. I'd been involved with the small press scene in Vermont that circled around Poet's Mimeo Cooperative (an aftershock of the San Francisco Renaissance in terms of its aesthetic location), then completed a low-residency M.F.A. at Vermont College (my dues paying to the longer traditions of lyric, narrative, and meditative poetry). But I was slow to emerge from the austere self-reliance I thought art demanded. Provincetown taught me that artistic and social purpose were allied. I'd come on a fellowship to the Fine Arts Work Center—ten artists and ten writers all young in our careers given the gift of seven months to live and work in studios once storage bins for Day's Lumber Yard. We were there because other artists and writers had seen the way the town was going—the days fading when someone could rent a shack, beg a fish from a trawler at the pier, hole up in the dunes for months with a notebook and pen.

As the economic profile of the town climbed, the prospects for writers and artists fell, especially those in the tenuous early stages who had neither cash reserves nor confidence in what they had accomplished or could envision. So Kunitz, Dugan, Judy Shahn, Robert Motherwell, Myron Stout, and the others said, Let's do something to keep this place good for art. But it wasn't just to keep the town interesting for themselves that they did it. Kunitz had lived many years in isolation after being unjustly denied (because he was a Jew) an academic position he deserved. Hard years followed, living in the boondocks doing journeyman's writing for reference books. The rejection and isolation didn't do much to nurture his art, he would later say, though it did teach him that a struggling writer needs not austere self-reliance but recognition and the companionship of like-minded others.

Provincetown also brought me closer to the subject of nature. Here was a culture, working fishermen and artists, shaped by terms nature had set. Certainly I'd lived more intimately with the wild huddled next to the Cold Hollow Mountains in Vermont. But here I found a counterpoint to that experience. The other fellows were mostly urban animals—lovers of film, libraries, museums, clubs, and all "the pleasures of the depraved animal" (as Milosz has stated, echoing Baudelaire). I began to see that relationship with nature is not a given, not the same for each person, but a result of character, shaped by family and culture and experience. How had my sense of nature been formed? Why did I feel so drawn to it? Why wasn't I terrified of nature, since I'd been attacked by dogs at a young age and knew what it felt like to be prey? Or was this experience the very reason I felt so intimately bonded with nature? The more I questioned, the more questions I found. I needed prose to ask and answer them—too much of a subject to handle with poetry alone. Why did intellectuals hold nature in disdain, as if wilderness were just a place to run to if you didn't have the guts for the city, as if the city were the only mirror complex enough in which to see your reflection? Why didn't everyone feel as I did that natural beauty raises the spiritual energy of the world? Why didn't everyone rise up in panic and rage at nature's ruin?

These questions made me feel as if my feet were stuck in sucking mud and my head was filled with black flies: to enter my ignorance meant going farther into the woods.

Tucson

You are right to require a conscious attitude from the artist toward his work, but you mix up two ideas: the solution of the problem, and the correct presentation of a problem. *Only the latter is obligatory for the artist. In "Anna Karenina" and "Onegin" not a single problem is solved, but they satisfy you completely just because all the problems are correctly presented.*

—Anton Chekhov

I'm living on a dirt road northeast of the city limits, just south of the Coronado National Forest and at the ankles of the Santa Catalina Mountains. It is the spring of 1999. Out my big picture windows I look up to the craggy bare ridge, slope speckled with saguaros and desert scrub. In the yard, bare dirt, one giant forked mesquite busy with Gila woodpeckers, and more saguaros, giant, many-branched elders that have presided over the scrub for more than one hundred years.

My place is a funky little studio, once a tack room, once a painter's workplace, once a daughter's hippie hangout, the landlady tells me. She's sorry she doesn't live in the attached house anymore. That's rented out too. I can tell from her readiness with the stories that she misses the life she had here. The main house was built in 1937, the tack room added in the 1960s. Once she owned sixty acres. There's an aerial photograph in the main house labeled "High Saguaro Ranch." Now she's down to four acres, and next door a new paved street bears the sign "High Saguaro Road," following the time-honored custom of developers to name new neighborhoods after what they destroy in building them. For a while the owner's then-husband ran helicopter tours over the Grand Canyon. I think that was when things were coming apart for her here. Now she's married to someone else and works in real estate in—Tennessee, is it, or Kentucky? It's hard to remember when all of our business has been by phone, fax, or electronic deposit.

She sounds happiest telling the older stories— how they bought the place in 1970 from the president of Kraft Foods, how his wife used the tack room for a studio, how his pal Perry Como liked to visit because they kept those small horses here, how she used to have big parties and play the piano and everyone sang. I can't imagine the place as an executive getaway. It has a rough, handbuilt look, painted saguaro rib pillars on the porch, mortar slopped into place adequate for the job but with no sign of the refined craftsmanship going into the stone walls in the new gated community climbing the hillside to the north. Maybe that's the point. This really was a getaway, a place to loosen the formalities of the working life, not a place to show off.

The exterior walls of the house and studio are desert stone flecked with mica and grained with quartz. One of my indoor walls is made of the same kind of stone, and one wall provides two picture windows that connect me with the desert's daily life. Each morning two rabbits hop across the yard, usually meeting the flock of Gambel's quail that skitter along like windup toys. Often there's a solitary roadrunner that stands still, staring, and several tiny verdins working the bark of the paloverde. In two months I've learned the difference, at last, between the Phainopepla and the Pyrrhuloxia.

And I've learned a great deal about the temperament of the latter, a wedge-headed cardinal-like bird, more gray than red and with a yellow bill. One determined male Pyrrhuloxia has discovered that a rival lives inside the sideview mirror of my car. Every morning at dawn he launches his attack, slamming his parrotlike bill into the glass again and again, wings in overdrive to keep up the assault until he retreats in exhaustion. The mirror is etched with his bill marks. It gives me pleasure, when stuck in the traffic jam I must endure twice a day in order to live here, seeing those battle scars on the glass and recognizing in them the futility of my anger.

My first night here I heard a scuffling in the gravel outside my door and opened it to find javelinas (collared peccaries) on the doorstep, a chorus of soft grunts that never quit, as if they could not move without vocalizing. Five of them in all, the two young ones hanging back in the darker night. The boar came close enough to sniff my hand, then recoiled. Again it approached, dared to take a whiff of me, then pulled away. Again—and this time I touched the coarse black bristles on his forehead, the snout bubblegum pink, hairless, gleaming with moisture and vented with big round flexing nostrils. Grunt, sniffle, shovel along the ground, circle, approach, and jerk away. And then they were gone.

Some nights the coyotes wail and yip. The sound is not what I expect, more chaotic and shrill, pack noise, never individuals. I wonder if they cry out excited over fresh kill, or just to hear their freedom heckle the night. When the noise quiets, a lone dog chained in a neighboring yard replies, its bark an unconvincing posture of ferocity set against that wilder song.

Some nights I hear the great horned owl—*hu-hu-hu-hoo!-hoo!*—and I pray for the rabbits in my yard. One night I heard paired owls in conversation outside my window. I was talking on the telephone with my lover, and ours was a conversation I did not want to have. And all through it, the tenderness and the crying and the pleas, I heard the owls say with no confusion *hu-hu-hu-hoo!-hoo!* and then came the long silence.

Desert night. When the moon is full, everything is so white I wake startled in the dark thinking it must have snowed. And when the moon is empty, the stars are so white and numerous I think, Who needs the moon anyway?

I'm living in the desert to see and hear these things before they are gone. There's no pretty way to say it. The desert is filling up with condos, mansions, and golf courses. An acre of Sonoran Desert, according to a January 1999 *High Country News* article, "much of it teeming with saguaro and prickly pear cacti and ironwood trees, disappears to development every two hours." Tucson has a strong community of artists, writers, scientists, and activists working for preservation and conservation, but so far every major zoning dispute over the past twenty-five years has been lost to developers. In the early 1970s the population of Tucson was 400,000; now it is 823,000 and growing. Another 400,000 people are expected to move to the metro area over the next twenty years. The city occupies a broad bowl surrounded by five mountain ranges, the sprawl climbing up the sides of the bowl. The total annual vehicle miles traveled in Tucson in 1970 was 2 million; in 1997, 16 million; expected in 2020, 28 million. Citizens have managed to prevent freeways from cutting through their urban neighborhoods. But this is a qualified victory, since the traffic is driving everyone, including at least one fervent Pyrrhuloxia, crazy.

> Number of rabbits, mice, rats, birds, and reptiles eaten by a typical Tucson housecat each year: 80.

> Number of toads, rabbits, snakes, lizards, small birds, javelinas, coyotes, and bobcats killed each year by automobiles in and around Saguaro National Park: 7,100.

Tucson's best hope for controlling sprawl is the proposed Sonoran Desert Conservation Plan. While it will take several more years to complete and implement, the plan is visionary in its scope, aimed at protecting not only sensitive habitat and ecological corridors, but also the cultural and historic characteristics that make the region unique, including ranches as well as historic and prehistoric sites. Development of course will not wait for the plan. Indeed, my fear is that developers will hasten to reap their profits before new restrictions come into play, blading away the desert and slapping together more and more colonies (picture them as bacteria on a culture plate) of the bland and placeless sameness that has come to mean economic progress in the "New West." In the foothills northwest of the city, developers have spent two years bulldozing land for a proposed development of nine thousand homes, four golf courses, and three resort hotels. If the Conservation Plan becomes a reality, growth in the desert will look quite different from this wholesale transformation of wilderness into a microburst of human habitation. Instead, we might see pockets of intense development interspersed with sprawling ironwood and saguaro forest; riverbeds long dry restored to flow through the city and floodplain, nourishing stands of mesquite, cottonwood, willow, and the wildlife they harbor; and archaeological sites illuminating the twelve thousand or so years that human beings have lived in this valley made prominent enough to eclipse a few golf courses—all in all a more gracious balance between people and the land, between our moment in history and those that precede and succeed us.

Through the scrub beyond my yard I see the flicker of earthmovers, blades, and pavers carving into the foothills above me. Already five monster homes lumber into my line of vision—houses bigger than anyone needs, houses that boast, "I've got mine and I'm closing the gate behind me." Paved driveways wind up the incline, transforming wild land into building lots. In another year or two, the hillside will be clustered with mansions lording it over the valley, an enclave of secessionists at peace with their safe little world behind walls, while in the city that twinkles like starlight, toxic waste piles up, homeless people sleep on the sidewalks, and young men "wearing colors" play at war, bleeding real blood on the streets. Do I just hate the monster homes and developments because their owners are rich and I am not? Aren't they entitled to their comfort, pleasure, and safety? I don't care if people build houses in the desert. I just want there to be some desert left after the houses are built. I want one person's comfort not to ride like a cement mixer on the back of another. I want to have some place to go where I can celebrate Creation without having to lament. I want to get beyond elegy. I want my love for natural beauty to be a force for protection, and I want art to be the form for my love.

My life in Tucson is filled with contingencies, and living on the outskirts is one of them. I did not come here to return to the austere reclusiveness of my earlier years. For all my love of nature, I spend most of my days indoors, as I have done for the past decade, working for a cultural institution. It's meaningful work, teaching writing and directing the University of Arizona Poetry Center, and it's what brought me to Tucson in 1990. When I first came to the desert, I wanted to live outside of the city and get to know the place through its wildness. I pictured a diminutive ranch with wagonwheels in the yard—something out of a Hopalong Cassidy movie. But I was forewarned by tales of sprawl and bought a city house five minutes from work. This winter, when my daughter and her family were casting about for a place to spend a few months refocusing—she on painting and he on letting go of his job as pastor of a liberal protestant church in Illinois—I offered them my house, thinking at last I'd seize my chance to get to know the rural neighbors—pocket gopher, scorpion, Gila woodpecker, and noble saguaro.

And I have gotten to know them within the context of my job, enjoying their company in my off-hours. I worry that I should be more of a conservation activist—piloting slow-growth initiatives, lobbying city hall, laying down my body (or at least my language) in the path of the pavers. But, as much as protection is my passion, it is not my profession, and I suffer as most people do trying to find the appropriate form for expressing what I believe so deeply. Instead of doing political action, I organize literary readings, send poets to teach in prisons and inner-city high schools, run a poetry library, and teach students how to write. I think of these tasks as cultural activism—nurturing lives devoted to creating meaning rather than to amassing things—because the crisis between our culture and its natural foundations is a crisis of beliefs and values at least as much as it is a crisis of policy and governance. Nevertheless, I feel inadequate as an opponent to the destruction I deplore when asked, as increasingly I am, to address grassroots environmentalists—professionals with their hands in the dirt of ecological restoration, nature education, conservation planning, and wildlands preservation. What good is a poem or an essay when nature is dying and we are to blame?

This frustration that the work of writing and cultural advocacy is not enough to protect the things we love was what led me to collaborate with Richard Nelson and Scott Russell Sanders in an open letter to readers of *Orion* magazine in 1995. The letter was a call to transform the terms of the public discussion about our way of life, our home places, and the fate of the earth. It was a complaint that the dialogue about how we inhabit the earth has been taken over by the voices of money and self-interest, the loudest among them talking "mostly about property rights, economic growth, and the right of individuals and corporations to pursue profit without restraint."

My frustration also called me to rethink my own role as an activist. I came of age during the era of three significant activist efforts: the civil rights movement, the antiwar (both Vietnam and nuclear) movement, and the women's liberation movement. These all erupted out of sleepy post–World War II complacency—the antiwar effort working to take apart social systems that were unjustifiably brutal, the civil rights and women's liberation movements to take apart systems of oppression that deny equal opportunity for all people. The nature of oppression is that it depletes the oppressed of hope and energy, awareness becoming dulled in order that one can endure. *It's just human nature to be brutal. We can't change things, so why try?*

I confess I never had much stomach for the combative mode of activism—though I did march in the spring 1968 Mobilization for Peace in New York City, and I had peacenik friends studying how to build bombs so that they could be more effective insurgents. Rather than trying to dismantle the existing social order, I tried to invent a new one, moving to a farm as far away from ground zero as I dared go, working in alternative schools and women's health clinics, learning how to be a self-respecting single mother, and writing poems on a homemade desk slapped together from an old barn door. Those actions felt more radical to me than pouring blood on Pentagon walls, because they gave me a sense of agency in my life—I was an actor (the star!) in the play of my life. That sounds woefully individualistic to me now that I know human culture is the most powerful evolutionary force on the planet, and that it is folly to think any individual can be separate from it, but my intentions then were broader. "Radical" meant working "at the root," making myself a better person, working from scratch to create cultural institutions that were more humane than the dominant ones. I'm thankful that others continued the public acts of demonstration. But I don't disavow my choices—they were in keeping with the goal of an artistic life: to wrest from the personal some form that speaks universally.

My work today follows that pattern, though what's changed is that I've found a satisfying role not only in art, but also in the cultural life of art—that is to say, I feel that my time is equally well spent in making art and in working to create a culture in which art can thrive. This kind of culture work can exact a toll, of course, on one's art practice. But it is important work to do, and particularly so if one can cultivate the perspective that neither of these two kinds of work is in opposition to the other. Rather, they are part of the whole in living out a commitment to art, an expression of one's citizenship. And I am convinced that it is a radically good thing to cultivate in others a commitment to artistic, intellectual, and spiritual pursuits. To give our inner lives the status of things, as Edward Sapir claims, is a step in the right direction for an overly acquisitive culture. Better to acquire a few more poems and prayers than a speedboat and plot in a subdivision on the bare flanks of Mt. Lemmon.

By now it will be apparent that geography has been a touchstone for my imagination, this essay having become so similar to other peregrinating works of mine—*Temporary Homelands* and *The Edges of the Civilized World*—for which travel has been a spur to keener attention and intimacy with place. "Touch-stone" is a word used almost exclusively these days for its metaphoric meaning—a thing which serves to test the genuineness or value of anything. The origin of this definition is mineral—a smooth dark stone used for testing the quality of gold and silver alloys by rubbing them against it and noting the color of the mark made on the stone. I know one of the pieties of nature writing says that one can only have intimacy with nature and form community by staying in one place, answering to it and for it against the culture's assaults. But when I have tested my own experience for its genuineness and value, I find that I have consistently deepened my understanding of the intricate weave between nature and culture by learning about them in different places. I consider it implausible that human culture will settle back into an agrarian way of life in which geographic mobility is shunned in the interest of staying put. Human beings are thrilled by the technological prowess that keeps them moving all over the planet and beyond. We are not going to stop these movements, unless, of course, disaster demands it of us. For those who wish to celebrate the agrarian way of life, I hold no antagonism. Indeed, there is much to admire in long study of one place. But what interests me, and what feels useful to me at this time in history, is to transpose what can be learned from more settled life-ways to the change and velocity of contemporary life. How, in a culture that is in love with its freedom and mobility, can individuals learn to conserve and preserve not only their own backyards but what is likely to become someone else's backyard in a year or two or twenty? The essay, poem, or story can become a paradigm for reestablishing the spiritual intimacy with nature that we have lost from lack of physical intimacy.

I know that mobility can instill an ethic of impermanence, of leaving one's mistakes and failures behind, rather than fixing them and fostering healing. But America is no longer an unsettled land, and as it grows more crowded, its membranes more permeable to the rest of the world, one finds that pulling up stakes and moving on leads one to face the same mistakes and failures played out in a new setting. We live in the same old story of fallibility and over-reaching goals that has been the bane and boon of human existence from the start. It does us good to face up to that—our stunning potential for messing things up—for without such awareness, we don't feel the need for restraint. And we do need mechanisms—morality and law, plans and paradigms—to restrain us, because it is in our nature to dominate, control, and succeed against the competition. For all of our goodness, we are not benign animals. In the first era of global exploration and colonization, human mobility was at its most heedless peak: Go wherever you want and claim it at whatever expense to local nature and culture. Today, human mobility is more democratic. Granted, galloping capitalism can turn a place into the economic colony of a few monster corporations. Nevertheless, our mobility has become less a way to run away from ourselves and more a way to see ourselves more clearly.

When I moved to Tucson in 1990, I had just begun to work in prose after writing poetry for twenty years. I had written an essay about Grand Manan and had realized in the writing how interested I was in the way the place and its people are one thing, as form and content are in a poem. I had also realized there was a good deal of content I wanted to explore that would require me to stretch out further into prose. And the questions I was asking at the time were all nourished by the move: How had my relationship with nature been shaped by family and culture? How does the human order fit into the larger natural order? How does nature act upon me as opposed to the dominant paradigm of people acting upon nature?

Of course, I fell in love with the West's magnificence, a scale and intensity of beauty that humbled me before its power. None of the sheltering blue hillsides, tidy seacoast villages, or fresh-mown velvet green pastures I was accustomed to swooning over in the Northeast. Here the mountains scraped up past the treeline to make their jagged statements to the sky. And the desert spanned into the shimmering edge of nowhere, its creatures adapting to harsh aridity with such inventive survival strategies that life seemed indomitable. Yes, there was sprawl, but in the spaces between the explosions of Sunbelt boom there was the serene and open space of wild land. That expansiveness invites a freedom of mind, I think, and makes one challenge old assumptions about the meaning of nature. The geologic nakedness of arid land gives a vivid sense that human power is small beneath that of the larger planetary forces. Whatever damage we inflict, one can easily think while gazing into the Grand Canyon's gullet that, in the long version of Earth's story, nature will endure.

I find it ironic that the stereotype of the Westerner is that of the rugged individualist, because my move to the West did more to make me understand myself as a cultural animal than to enhance my sense of independence. As a member of the dominant cultural group, I do not often see my whiteness, which is particularly invisible to me when I move in the monochromatic social circles of my Eastern roots. But Tucson, like much of the West, is culturally permeable, and here I have had the chance to learn from a place where Mexican and Native American people give definition to the community. And that has made me more apparent, often humblingly so, to myself. Not only is our mass culture one that denies the fact of ecological disaster. It is also a culture that denies the fact of cultural inequity and the ferocious wounds that the European conquest inflicted upon America's indigenous people.

My ancestors, as civic leaders in Puritan New England, had a hand in inflicting those wounds. One incident in particular haunts me. I learned of it only recently while researching family history for an article on the Salem witch trials. William Hathorne, a distinguished soldier in King Phillip's War (1675–76), made his fortune in one day when he captured four hundred peaceful Indians who had gathered in Dover, New Hampshire, for trade and festivities. He arranged a ruse, telling them about a game his people used to play in England. The Indians should pretend to attack the soldiers and then the fun would start. When the game began in earnest, the Indians were captured and sorted out by strength and size like so much timber, with two hundred of the strongest chained body to body and loaded into slave ships that carried them to Bermuda to be sold. The crime earned the young soldier and his business partner close to a million dollars, and he was celebrated in a sermon by Cotton Mather for his bravery in inflicting such a stunning wound upon the savages.

I am deeply ashamed and sorry that my ancestors had a hand in these injustices, even more so because they were respected and pious civic leaders. This is a terrible grief we all must carry, a terrible remorse at human cruelty and blindness, now that we know more about the crimes committed by our own ancestors—and everyone else's—than did any other people in history. It is easy to feel compassion for the victims. But how do I feel compassion for my own ancestors? How do I honor and respect my elders when I am ashamed of them? The only way is to face up to them, to name the evil they did as evil, and to acknowledge that the capacity for evil lies in everyone. They were victims of the time in which they lived, blind to the injustices they caused. We too must be blind. When I try to imagine the deeds for which our descendents will find it most difficult to forgive us, I am quite convinced that it will be our cavalier destruction of the natural world.

In 1997, I was asked by the Orion Society to lead a conversation at the colloquium convened in honor of Gary Snyder when he received the John Hay Award for his writing and activism. My assignment was to address the question, Does activism compromise one's art? The question was very American, as Snyder pointed out. In Europe and Asia an artist is a public person—seeing the responsibility to use some of his or her skills on behalf of society. I answered the question by saying, Yes, of course compromise occurs. The work of activism exhausts us and makes us grieve; it takes us from our studios; it makes us scholars, negotiators, combatants, administrators, and business heads when we would prefer to be makers, dreamers, healers, and dancers. And if art is made to serve our activism, it can lose its elemental engagement with the unknown; its freedom to be outrageous, obscure, absurd, and wild; its need is to speak the truth as it cannot be spoken in political discourse.

Asking this question is like asking, Does culture compromise nature? Does love compromise solitude? Does eating compromise prayer? Does the mountain compromise the sky? All of these are relationships of complementarity, correspondence, call-and-response, the mutualistic whole of existence. Gathering in Snyder's home place, listening to stories of the Yuba Watershed Institute and the building of the Ring-of-Bone Zendo, and celebrating the poet's work provided a lesson in how radical an act it is in this culture to live a life devoted to something other than capitalism. Yes, we all participate in it. Yes, we are all complicit in environmental degradation and overconsumption simply because of our position in the global food chain. But we can make life choices that nurture more meaningful and sustainable relationships. To live a life devoted to art, to spiritual practice, to service to one's community and ecosystem, restores faith in our collective human enterprise. Work on the culture is work on the self.

Art can serve activism by teaching an attentiveness to existence and by enriching the culture in which our roots are set down. Culture is both the crop we grow and the soil in which we grow it. And human culture is the most powerful evolutionary force on Earth these days. The grief we feel at abuses of human power is the first positive step toward transforming that power for the good. Legislation, information, and instruction cannot effect change at this emotional level—though they play a significant role. Art is necessary because it gives us a new way of thinking and speaking, shows us what we are and what we have been blind to, and gives us new language and forms in which to see ourselves. To effect profound cultural change requires that we educate ourselves about our own interior wildness that has led us into such a hostile relationship with the forces that sustain us. Work on the self is work on the culture.

The reciprocating relationship between self and

culture was brought home to me recently when Chinese dissident poet Bei Dao came to Tucson to give a poetry reading. Considered by many to be China's foremost poet of the prodemocracy period, Bei Dao is currently living in exile in the United States, his work accused of inciting the Tiananmen Square uprising in 1989. He spoke informally with students and local poets about Chinese writing during the past thirty years. He was in high school, seventeen years old, when the Cultural Revolution began. His formal education ended and he became a member of the Red Guard. In 1969 he was sent several hundred miles south of Beijing to work. He was a construction worker there for eleven years. In the countryside he discovered poverty and backward conditions, seeing how different life was from the propaganda he'd been given, and he lost his enthusiasm for the revolution. Then he began to study literature and to write.

Books were banned, except those speaking the official discourse of the state, such as books on Marxism and Mao's thought. Bei Dao and his friends read whatever they could get their hands on—books stolen from closed libraries or banned books confiscated from houses: classical Chinese poetry, Lorca, Kafka, *Catcher in the Rye*.

Bei Dao founded the magazine *Jintian (Today)* published from 1978 to 1980 during the Democracy Wall movement, when people who had suffered during the Cultural Revolution came to the capital to express their dissatisfaction. *Jintian* was the first unofficial literary magazine published in China since the Communist takeover in 1949. The first issue's sixty pages were posted on the Wall, with blank sheets of paper beneath each printed page so that readers could let the editors know what they thought. The magazine was also distributed to various cultural organizations in Beijing—publishing houses, universities, and literary institutes. There was tremendous excitement about this new writing, and poetry groups sprouted up all over the place.

"Writing was a forbidden game," Bei Dao explained, "that could cost one one's life." The poetry they published amounted to a new language, since "for thirty years in the Chinese language there had been no personal voice at all."

The official line on Bei Dao's poetry was that it was politically subversive because it expressed intimate thoughts, asserting the rights of the individual to his or her own private experience. And the more obscure Bei Dao's poems became, the more subversive the authorities considered him. What struck me most profoundly was how different this notion of the political was from the sensibility of most poets in the United States. For us, aesthetic subjectivity is considered an escape from politics. In Bei Dao's experience of Communist China, subjectivity has meant entering the political arena.

Once an interviewer asked Bei Dao to comment on his statement that "poets must not exaggerate their own function, but even less should they underrate themselves." He replied, "On the one hand poetry is useless. It can't change the world materially. On the other hand it is a basic part of human existence. It came into the world when humans did. It's what makes human beings human."

That language is a key tool for cultural change is evident in the long story of human evolution and in the short one of Mao's Cultural Revolution as well as in the manipulations of advertisement and the affirmations of prayer: language makes us the speed-learners among species, and this power can be used to good or ill. All good literature helps to renew language—to restore its capacity to link the inner life with outer experience, and to sing the song of the soul on the stage of history. And environmental literature, at least since Rachel Carson's *Silent Spring*, has had a remarkably tangible impact on both the ethics and the politics of conservation. This literature has created a common language with which to bear witness to, praise, and lament our wounded relationship with nature. It has made more sensuous, and therefore more real, our increasingly abstracted relationship with flora and fauna. It has made invaluable discoveries of science accessible to readers untrained in scientific disciplines, discoveries central both to understanding our predicament and to finding remedies for it. It has served as a collective act of preservation for places lost, lifeways lost, species and cultures lost, forests and mountainsides and rivers lost, and faith in our own kind lost.

I don't mean to say that when a forest is gone you can replace it with a poem. When a forest is gone, you cannot replace it. But with written words you can bear witness, you can hold a memory of the forest for others to experience and celebrate, you can grieve over the loss and rage against the forces that have leveled the forest—and through grief you can fall in love with forests again, and through that falling you can believe again in the human capacity for love and in the faith that we might learn to protect what we love.

Poamoho

I'm no longer at all sure where to draw the line between art and nature, Becoming and Origin.

—John Berger

The heart thinks constantly.

—*The I Ching*

The message on my machine said the hike would be moderate, mostly level, a group of high school kids led by Steve Montgomery, the naturalist I had recently met at an environmental education conference in Honolulu. Great, I thought, eager to get farther into the rain forest and especially to do so guided by an expert on bugs. Steve had discovered some twenty new species of insects. His business card sported a photographic image of "killer caterpillar new species 8"—a micro Godzilla captured in the act of consuming a fly. Being a bit bug crazy myself after a decade-long affair with monarch butterflies, I knew that he and I had a lot in common. We had exchanged bug books—his gallery of bug mugshots in *Hawaiian Insects and Their Kin* and my poem sequence *The Monarchs*. He had the cheerful good humor of one who loves his work and sees the comic aspect of it. I wasn't wrong in thinking he'd be good company in the woods, but I had no idea that the lesson I'd learn on the hike would be so close to the edge, literally, of life, that it would have more to do with the spiritual than the terrestrial domain.

Then again, in the Hawaiian Islands, the spiritual and terrestrial are never far apart. Traditional Hawaiians call spiritual energy "mana," and for them it is present in people, animals, plants, and rocks. It demands respect. The old beliefs came with wayfinders who sailed here in great outrigger canoes, navigating by stars and wave patterns, from the Marquesas and Society Islands. Their culture was guided by a complex hierarchy of gods and ancestral spirits who entered into all aspects of daily life. Sacred stories, some taking more than a year to tell, conveyed the history of ancestors to the community, and chants carried prayers and offerings to gods and guardian spirits, among them the *'aumākua* (guardian god) of a family into which a divine offspring was born, providing the family with special protection and requiring special reverence. According to scholar Martha Beckwith, the *'aumākua* could take the form of an animal or plant or other natural object and could grant more-than-natural powers to family members because of their sacred descent. As contemporary as much of Hawaiian life has become in recent years, the echoes of old beliefs can be heard everywhere in the islands. During my months of living there, I sought out those echoes. At times it seemed they sought out me.

I had come to Oahu to teach at the University of Hawai'i and to cast about for a new research question. For the past decade I'd shaped my writing projects loosely around the process of carrying a question around with me for a few years to see how various places would help me answer it. For *Temporary Homelands* the question had been, How have family and culture shaped my relationship with nature? For *The Monarchs* it was somewhat more vague, as perhaps is fitting for a poem sequence, a form that resists coming to conclusions. After visiting the winter roosts of monarch butterflies in coastal California, I became fascinated with the animal, wanting to learn everything I could about it. I dove into field study, library research, reflection, and imaginative association. I apprenticed myself to the monarchs, trying to understand how they lived their lives and how their existence might inform mine. From the start the project announced itself as a sequence. I was reading William Carlos Williams's sequence *Paterson,* a work informed by the metaphoric assumption that a man is a city. My metaphoric assumption was that a woman is a fragile migratory bug smart enough to find her way safely in the world. But that simplifies the matter. The research question that complicated the project concerned the nature of intelligence. What forces guide the life of a monarch butterfly and what do they have to teach me about the forces that guide human lives?

With the book I'd just finished, *The Edges of the Civilized World,* the question announced itself early in the writing, even though the answer can only be a process of unfolding: Can we restore faith in civilization as an expression of radical hope in the best of the collective human enterprise on Earth—those acts and accomplishments that honor beauty, wisdom, understanding, justice, inventiveness, love, and moral connection with others?

In Hawai'i the question that began to form is this: How can I authentically speak about my experience of the sacred in nature when I do not feel connected spiritually or intellectually with a tradition, such as that of native Hawaiians, that grounds its beliefs in nature? My faith lineage begins with childhood in an agnostic family—my mother a lapsed Christian Scientist who enjoyed reading about such religious exotica as the Hunzas of Kashmir, and my father a man who found the ritual of Communion too cannibalistic to inspire his faith and refused at age fifteen to return to any church. As a teenager I developed a weak alliance with the West Avon Congregational Church (I joined so that I could sing duets in the choir with my best friend). I practiced meditation for five years so that I could walk in step with a contemplative boyfriend. I dabbled in church-going, various liberal denominations, but never felt a deeply shared sense of spiritual hunger in those congregations. More often I felt a constraining sense of propriety when what I longed for was to give myself to joyful lamentation in the presence of—the mere invitation to—the divine. I've read broadly (if not as deeply as disciplined spiritual practice may require)— Hinduism, Taoism, Confucianism, Native American-ism, Tiellard de Chardin, Thomas Berry, Annie Dillard,

Carl Jung, Simone Weil, Saint Augustine. The most auspicious evidence I can offer for the seriousness of my spiritual quest is a thirty-year relationship with *The I Ching,* the ancient Chinese *Book of Changes,* lauded by Jung as "the right book" for "lovers of wisdom," though "like a part of nature, it waits until it is discovered." The book offers neither facts nor power nor causal explanation, but rather teaches an abiding relationship with the forces of change and chance that govern nature and the human spirit.

I take comfort in knowing that I'm not alone in this feeling of being a spiritual orphan. I take comfort in the words of Karen Armstrong, who left the Catholic convent after seven years because she found the church's definition of God too arrogant for her faith. People are turning away from God, she reports. In the United Kingdom only thirty-five percent of people say they believe in God. She thinks that number is optimistic. Churches have stood empty and now are becoming restaurants, theaters, warehouses, and private homes. The god who once presided there, she says, died in Auschwitz. If God existed, how could he remain unmoved and powerless over such atrocities? But God is not a being. To say that God does not "exist" violates nothing, because "existence" refers to the dimension we are able to perceive, and "God" refers to a whole other level. Jews and Christians were once called atheists by their pagan contemporaries because their concept of the divine was so new. The Sufi mystics said that each one of us is an unrepeatable expression of the divine, therefore each one of us will know God in an entirely different manner.

"We are not," Armstrong says, "like dogs. We cannot just relax into existence. Dogs do not worry what happens after death or what is happening now to dogs in other parts of the world." Ever since our ancestors climbed out of the trees, we have needed art and religion to get to the gut level of our being. Even lacking a definition, we know the terror and wonder of what stirs in us below the rational, beyond our control, what wounds us into prayer and compassion. One may catch glimpses, moments of insight may flicker against moments of doubt, one may feel the dimension of the sacred in one's life, but "God" lies beyond our human conception.

What is God? I do not know. I am deeply religious and deeply skeptical of religion. "You are a pagan," a friend once told me, "because you see deity not just *in* things, but *as* things."

So, when I got the call from Steve about the hike, I put on my shorts and bright white new sneakers, slipped my lunch, rainslicker, and pocket notebook into my daypack, and drove up to Kamehameha High School to meet the *Hui Lama* (hiking club). The school is dedicated to educating children of native Hawaiian descent. I was almost the last to arrive. The others were assembled in the parking lot, a dozen or so teenagers, a few teachers and parents, all dressed in long pants and the rugged gear one wears knowing one's going to get dirty. Two ROTC boys dressed in camouflage fatigues with loops of climbing rope strung to their belts looked me over. I must have been a sorry sight, a *haole* (the Hawaiian equivalent to "gringo") dressed for a stroll in the park. Biology teacher Chuck Burrows—a muscular man who'd been leading student hikes for something like fifty years, giving new vigor to anyone's notion of the elderly, a loved man, one could tell, from the way people spoke his name—handed me a permission slip so cautionary it seemed more appropriate for bungee jumping than a hike in the woods. Details emerged bit by bit, pebbles in the flow of conversation. Our destination was Poamoho, a region in the Koolau Range northwest of Honolulu. A fourteen-mile hike to the summit and back. To get to the trailhead we needed permits from Dole Pineapple and the United States Army, both of which control a surprisingly large amount of land on Oahu. I signed my name, dismissing the climbing ropes as macho excess, though I began to realize that the idea of a "moderate hike" for a man who has searched the wilderness throughout the Pacific Islands for undiscovered bugs might lean a bit closer to "rigorous" in my guidebook of this day.

I was assigned to ride with the only other person wearing shorts, Keawe, a young man teaching Hawaiian language and culture at the university. I may have been *haole* and he *kama'aina,* but we were clearly the items to circle in the drawing titled "What doesn't fit in this picture?" So we climbed into his little pickup truck and joined the caravan heading for the hills.

"Are you named after the tree?" I ask, thinking *kiawe,* the acacia.

He laughed, then frowned.

"That's what everyone says. No, after an important man in my ancestry, a chief on the Big Island."

He did not belong to the hiking club, but was a graduate of Kamehameha High School and had asked if he could come along because he had a special quest. He was happily engaged to be married. But he had dreamed of finding a white lehua flower. The red lehua blooms on the ohia tree, but a white blossom on that tree would be very rare indeed. He had sought out two interpretations of the dream, one from his grandmother, if I recall correctly, and one from another respected elder. One reading of the dream said that he had already found his white lehua in his fiancée; but the other said that he must go and find the flower in order to win her.

We compared notes on the upcoming hike. He too had expected an easy go of it.

"Fourteen miles?" he asked, blanching at the prospect. "Did you see those ropes?"

"Someone said it's the same route up and back, so we can stop and wait, if we wear out." I said this to console myself as much as him.

We compared notes on the ROTC boys and our shorts, admitting we hadn't prepared for paramilitary action. And we drove on to reconvene with the caravan at the Dole Pineapple Visitor's Center. Some other kids and a father, head of the local fire department, joined us. The father too carried ropes. Keawe and I exchanged glances, and we climbed back into the cars, trucks, and vans to wind along dirt roads through pineapple fields at the base of the finned green mountains. The dirt was slick from the previous night's rain. We fishtailed and skittered, took wrong turns then right ones, until we came to a rutted red dirt turnout just into the woods. It was too wet to go on, so we unloaded and prepared to hike the last mile of road to the trailhead.

Chuck convened the group into a circle where we stood and introduced ourselves one at a time. The students said where they lived and what grade they were in. Steve said, "I'm in grade fifty-one," and everyone laughed. Chuck asked Keawe to tell the special reason why he had joined us for the day. Then Chuck said we should listen to the sounds of the birds and winds when we entered the forest, and we would be with our ancestors. He asked Keawe to give us a chant, and the visceral music of it bound us. He asked him to tell us what it meant. Keawe said that he had asked permission for us to go into the forest and for us to go safely.

Steve led us on the way up the Poamoho Trail, and we followed in single file into the woods, stopping to learn things he knew along the way. Prehistoric banana tree. *Pinao*, the largest dragonfly in America (though I wondered later had I confused this in my notes with *Pinao ula*, the endemic red damselfly?). *Hame* (welcome), orange berries. *Loulu*, the fan palm, the only palm native to Hawai'i. He pointed across the steep valley to the opposite ridge—the royal palm, which has no dispersal agent here so had to be planted, a native of the Florida Everglades. Then Steve ran on ahead, slipping and sliding in the mud, eager to get to the next fascination. He wore Japanese reef slippers—better than sneakers or hiking boots, he said, on rain-slicked jungle trails—and green combat pants with big pockets. The trail rose into the green folding cliffs, ridges bending and rippling into one another, rising to one side of us and falling to the other, and we hiked along the edges or over the tops of the cliffs, everything softened with lush foliage so that it was easy to forget the height and steepness always at our sides. When we approached a fallen rotting tree downslope of the trail, Steve stumbled willingly down through the scrub into the composting mulch. We learned that this was the characteristic behavior of the creature, the denser the scrub the more likely he'd slither and clamber and tuck his way into it, disappearing for pregnant minutes, then reemerging with a grin and a clear plastic pill bottle boasting his find. This time it was a tiny spider carrying a pearly white egg case on her back. He handed me the vial.

"You want to carry this for me?" And I nestled the treasure in my pack.

Back on the trail, he led us on. There were ferns clustered in the crotch of a tree—their name meaning "Woman who sits on the mountain." There was *aha kea,* in the coffee family, its yellowish wood the traditional material for the gunwales of canoes. When a boat builder uses another wood, he paints the gunwales yellow. There was *Clidemia* and more *Clidemia* (Koster's curse), the South American weed that wages chemical warfare with other plants by stopping them from germinating. In some places there was nothing else growing, though insects had been brought in to control it. In others, strawberry guava from Brazil spilled its fruit all over the trail. The Chinese leafhopper sucked sap from one hundred different kinds of plants, its saliva toxic to many of them. Researchers were looking for a wasp to attack the invader and restore the balance. There was the *olapa* tree (Chuck looked over my shoulder to help with the spelling of Hawaiian words); and the *akia* plant producing a neurotoxin used for catching fish, the weed thrown into a tidepool and fish gathered up with a scoop net; and *uluhe* ferns, spreading over the island for the past two and a half million years and covering the steep cliffsides, the first plant to grow after a landslide and called with affection the "forest Band-Aid."

The higher in altitude we climbed, the more dispersed became our group and the thinner the vegetation. The square-stemmed mintless mint and New Zealand tea and *uki* grass. The higher we got, the wetter and stonier the trail became. The mountain we climbed was a shield volcano, its summit in the altitude most favored by Oahu's daily rain clouds. Gullies had been eroded in the trail, and narrow slot canyons were filled with soupy red-brown water. We were all soaked to the knees already when the rains and winds came, pelting us as we puffed up the last stretch to the summit. The ROTC boys joked, "If the Viet Cong don't get you, the leptospirosis will." Steve had long since left us in favor of bugs.

As we neared the summit, I was in the lead, breaking out of the last passage of thin forest into the rolling grassy, wind-whipped meadow. Ahead I spotted a plant that stood as tall as a cornstalk, a single spiky magenta blossom capping it like a crown.

"There's a really strange looking plant up here," I called back to the group.

"Show Chuck," someone answered.

I stepped aside, so that he could be the first to get close to it.

"Oh, that's the lobelia. *Koli'i.* That's what we come up here to see."

We saw it. Then went on, the wind and the rain now so fierce no one wanted to linger. From the summit we could see the Pacific to the north and far below. We could see that sunlight was meeting the beach, though here the tempest made us each seek a leeward shelter. How could it be so cold and harsh at a mere three thousand feet in the tropics? The kids whirled and raced in the wind. Those of us who were older shuddered and leaned into ourselves for warmth. I turned my back on the lookout and found the sheltered backside of a hillock, joining two teachers who sat and pried their way with icy fingers into the sandwiches and cookies they'd brought for lunch. Everyone was soaked from head to foot, and after sitting for ten minutes in the wind no one looked happy, and the group began to disperse by twos and threes and fours heading back down the trail to warmth. I was sitting with Debbie, and we'd been telling our stories—she'd come to Hawai'i as a Navy wife, had kids, then divorced, now was a science teacher at the high school and trying hard to make her life work out. I did not know her, but I knew she was not really *in* her life, the way one is when it feels that one's choices fit. I knew she was still trying on her fate, that she did not yet love it. How could I know such a thing about a stranger? Forgive me if I am mistaken—so many ways it is possible to get the world wrong.

She was quiet, staring at the knee of her wet jeans where a dopey bee staggered along. She set her palm beside it like a little boat, and the bee walked on board. She held it close to her face and admired it, then showed it closely to me.

"It doesn't belong up here," she said. "It's way too cold. I wish I had some way to take it down with us."

I remembered the plastic eyeglass case in my backpack and pulled it out. We popped the bee inside, and I tucked the case into my pack.

Debbie and I made the descent together, the others dispersed ahead or behind, and occasionally we'd intersect with some of them but seemed to keep ending up alone. We talked about work and marriage and mothering—our disappointments and our hopes. We helped each other over the gullies and savored guavas when our water ran out. Our legs were sore, muscles wasted and tense, our clothes and hair soaked; one or the other of us kept slipping and falling on slick mud or stone, and there was ridiculous joy in being so dirty and sweaty and exhausted together as we hiked farther from the stormy summit and deeper into sun-mottled forest. I might have preferred to hear more of the wind and birdsong in those last miles of wilderness, but our talking went on, and I gave myself to it.

We were within a quarter mile of the trailhead when she fell, though we didn't know where we were at the time. For miles we'd been encouraging each other, "We're almost there now." We were long past the most perilous passages of the trail—here was level ground, an easy curve, a wide pathway. A relaxed weedy cliff rose to our right, and to our left a steep fern-covered cliff descended out of sight. One minute she was walking a few feet ahead of me, and the next she was falling head first over the edge.

"It was the strangest thing," I later told Keawe, "as if some force came along and threw her over the cliff."

"There are powers in the mountains," he'd said. "We call them the home of the gods."

Even more strange to me was my response to Debbie's falling. I stepped up to the edge and looked down. I could see her, just barely, through the ferns and scrub, clinging to the nubby cliffside, maybe twenty feet below.

"Are you all right?" I called down.

"I think so," she said, though her breath was shallow and fast with panic. *No problem*, I thought, though I wasn't really thinking this, because clearly this really *was* a problem. I was feeling it—a calm washing through my body that made me certain everything was all right. Whether I say that the calm was a physiologic response—endorphins perhaps pumped up by the danger—or whether I say that the calm was holy spirit—a more-than-human power—flowing into my body does not matter. The fact is that a woman clung for her life to a cliffside, and I was certain and calm, and both of these facts were beyond my control. I leaned over the edge to hear her whispering Hail Mary's between hyperventilating gasps. Below her the cliff fell another fifty feet or so, then met a seam where another cliff joined it, and the crease between the two ferny basaltic walls fell far below toward the tiny stream that laced through the distant valley floor.

"We'll get you up, don't worry," I said. "Try to breathe slowly. Try to hold on." And I looked around me for anything that would tell me what to do. And when I looked, I found a tree limb that had fallen in the trail, and I thought I could reach her with it, knowing she could not hold on long to wet rock and ferns. I lowered the limb to her.

"Brace as much of your weight as you can against the rock," I said, thinking, How can I hold her? What if I feel myself starting to fall? I kneeled on the trail, braced a knee against the slight mound of a protruding rock—surely not enough resistance to hold me, but it did, as I centered my body's gravity over the earth rather than the chasm.

For how long did we struggle there, reaching and

grasping and praying and calling for help? Maybe twenty minutes. Maybe thirty. Maybe forever. I was fearless and I have no idea why. I thought calmly—after she'd said, I can't hold on anymore, after I'd felt the weight of her pulling me closer to falling, after I'd said, I'm not going to leave you, after we'd gotten her close enough to let the limb fall and grip each other's wrists, after we'd each said, Wait, I don't think I can hold on anymore, after we'd both called out, Dear Jesus help us—I thought calmly, What will I do if I feel myself going over? Will I let her go? And I thought calmly, Yes, I will let her go.

What horrifies me is the calmness with which I decided to let her life go out of my hands if saving her meant giving my own. But that was only thinking. I did not let her go. I was stronger than it was possible for me to be, and so was she. The thought of making the other choice gave me strength I did not know I had. At the last moment of our strength, her elbows now braced over the lip of the cliff, one of the ROTC boys came running, finally hearing our cries. He bristled with energy, leaned over the edge, grabbed her by the belt and heaved her body up onto the ground. She wept there for a while, lying on her stomach. I stroked her back, and then we walked down to the trailhead.

The others who had preceded us were standing around eating snacks and drinking sodas, wiping mud off their boots and putting on dry T-shirts, if they had them. Debbie tried to tell them what had happened, but no one seemed sufficiently impressed for her to feel they understood.

"She won't be happy," one of her colleagues joked, "unless we say it's the biggest thing that's happened since Princess Di was killed."

But one of the Hawaiian kids heard her, a quiet boy who stood with us to listen and talk.

"Were there any animals around when this happened?" he asked.

"No, I don't think so," I said. Then I remembered the bee I still carried in my eyeglass case. Debbie and I stared at each other, as if we'd seen something invisible. She leaned over and pulled her jeans up over her calf to reveal her bee tattoo.

"Bees have always been very special to me," she said.

"That's amazing," I said, though I wasn't sure what I meant.

"Not really," the kid said. "That kind of thing happens all the time."

I knew then he was thinking that the bee was her 'aumākua—a fact as apparent to him as life-saving endorphins had been to me and the Holy Mother of Jesus had been to Debbie. Maybe it was not our belief that an animal or bug could give a person special protection, but it seemed as plausible as anything we could imagine. Maybe we didn't really believe that, but the bee was so integral a part to the pattern that was the day, we could not dismiss it, any more than we could dismiss the tree limb or the grip of our own hands. Meaning, like the sacred, is present if you look for it, but absent if you do not.

I dug the eyeglass case from my backpack and released the sleepy passenger. It wasn't until the next day when I woke up with my back and arms aching that I remembered the spider carrying her egg case, which I also had brought down from the mountain. I called Steve and asked him what to do with her, and he told me where to find the research lab on campus. I went there and handed the pill bottle over to a woman in a lab coat.

"I'm sorry it took so long for me to get her here. I hope she's okay," I said.

"Oh, she looks just fine," said the woman admiringly, and I handed over my charge.

I went to the library to research Hawaiian legends, to see if historical texture would add anything to my understanding of the remarkable events on Poamoho. I read some ancient stories, complex genealogies, and myths. But they did not help, because as rich as they were, they were not my story.

I'd been looking for a way to talk about the sacred that was authentically mine. What had I learned on that day? What was the ground note of its music? Bugs, I thought. Steve's more-than-twenty discoveries and my one apprenticeship to monarchs that had brought us together, the insects collaborating with scientists to restore balance within a besieged botanical system, Debbie's real and tattooed bees, and the spider carrying her egg case into the lab—all parts of the pattern that was the day, parts of the whole that is not perceivable because, as John Steinbeck wrote, "the pattern goes everywhere and is everything and cannot be encompassed by finite mind or by anything short of life—which it is." Bugs, I thought, on whose backs the world rides, unlike human beings who ride so heavily on Earth's back. Bugs, the smallest perceivable part of the biological whole. The world would be fine if people became extinct, but without bugs, the basic work they do of pollination, decomposition, stirring up the soil, and cleaning up everyone's mess with their fastidious appetites, Earth would become a barren dirty rock.

In my story I may not know how to define the sacred, but I have felt its presence in nature and in the coming-into-form that is language and art. I have felt it in the space inside the body and in the space between the stars. What holds the Creation together? Not emptiness. Without the health of the smallest among us, we could not exist.

Alison Hawthorne Deming

A PORTRAIT

by Scott Slovic

Who would you want to be with in a moment of crisis? Who would you want to be paying attention as the world burns? Say you had a choice between a poet and a plumber—an intellectual-aesthete and a person who puts things together and makes sure they work. Somewhere, at this moment, the world is in flames. Perhaps the smoke is not visible. Perhaps the "burning" exists only in the chemical-filled drinking water running through your pipes, or in the faint plume of dust at the edge of town, marking the insidious sprawl of tract homes and mansions. Whose help should you call for? Poet or plumber, firefighter or activist? I would maintain that perhaps there's not such a big difference among these choices.

Again and again, the image from Poamoho flashes before my eyes. The poet and her companion make their way down the trail on a knife-edge ridge, overgrown with tropical foliage, and then the companion suddenly steps off the edge and screams for help. The poet, amused by her own intellect and distracted by images of green and blue, could well have merely gasped and lamented—alas, poor friend lost to the dangers of a mountain. Instead, each time I replay the scene in my imagination (guided by the *Credo* narrative), the poet leaps into action, assesses her companion's condition, discerns a practical solution, and rescues the other woman. The poet, shaken and shocked by the near tragedy, later records the experience in words—but at the time of the fall, when action is required, she acts.

How to mine such an experience for meaning? Here, too, pragmatism and common sense are required. The philosopher and nature writer Kathleen Dean Moore compares the essayist to an osprey. This bird of prey, famous for its graceful coasting above rivers and lakes and its dramatic dives into near-opaque water, talons outstretched for the crucial death grip, will glide and glide and glide, waiting for just the right moment when riffled, murky water suddenly becomes transparent enough to reveal fish—and then the osprey folds its wings and drops like a ball of lead . . . with talons. These talons, though, have evolved to grip but not to release, a convenient enough talent if the captured fish is of an appropriate size. But sometimes the osprey pierces the water only to sink its talons into an enormous body from which there is no surfacing. The essayist, too, according to Moore, hovers and soars, waiting for the world's water to become momentarily transparent, and then she dives. Sometimes experiences are too heavy for prose.

At times like this, it is helpful if the writer has access not only to the essayist's powers of analysis and explanation, but to the poet's register of symbolism and imagery. Alison Hawthorne Deming, transferring back and forth between poetry and prose (and sometimes merging the two), is such a writer. Her work demonstrates a unique—and pragmatic—flexibility, an awareness of the precise effects of lyricism and discursive explanation, of story and analysis. These complementary modes of language recur throughout her work, in a way that fits the purposes of the moment.

Pragmatism, competence, confidence. The certainty of figuring something out, getting something done— solving problems, turning a phrase just right. One of my favorite examples of pragmatic behavior in American literature appears in Thoreau's chapter "The Ponds" in *Walden:*

> Once, in the winter, many years ago, when I had been cutting holes through the ice in order to catch pickerel, as I stepped ashore I tossed my axe back on to the ice, but, as if some evil genius had directed it, it slid four or five rods directly into one of the holes, where the water was twenty-five feet deep. Out of curiosity, I lay down on the ice and looked through the hole, until I saw the axe a little on one side, standing on its head, with its helve erect and gently swaying to and fro with the pulse of the pond; and there it might have stood erect and swaying till in the course of time the handle rotted off, if I had not disturbed it. Making another hole

directly over it with an ice chisel which I had, and cutting down the longest birch which I could find in the neighborhood with my knife, I made a slip-noose, which I attached to its end, and, letting it down carefully, passed it over the knob of the handle, and drew it by a line along the birch, and so pulled the axe out again.

I think of this passage from *Walden* in connection with Alison Deming's life and work, because she's the sort of person who would figure out a way to retrieve her axe from the pond's bottom, too, instead of throwing up her hands and lamenting the tool's fate. The Tucson chapter of her *Credo* essay addresses this impulse to act directly and concretely in response to perceived problems in the world. "What good is a poem or an essay when nature is dying and we are to blame?" she writes. The next paragraph explains her collaboration with Richard Nelson and Scott Russell Sanders to address readers of *Orion* magazine and call for an ecological bill of rights and responsibilities, with Aldo Leopold's land ethic—"A thing is right when it tends to preserve the integrity, stability, and beauty of the biotic community. It is wrong when it tends otherwise"—serving as the first principle. As three practitioners of literary language, the writers exhort the community of environmental thinkers and artists to "find more effective means of influencing government and industry and individuals. We must work to transform the terms of public discussion about our way of life, about our home places, about the fate of the earth, and about our membership in the great living community that contains us all." Deming's effort to use her voice toward a transformative effect on society, working together with close friends and colleagues, is the environmentalist equivalent of Thoreau's retrieval of his axe.

John Dewey, the eminent philosopher from the movement known as "pragmatism," writes that "any practical activity will, provided that it is integrated and moves by its own urge to fulfillment, have esthetic quality." A stone rolling downhill, adhering to the forces of nature and moving toward the fulfillment of its ultimate resting place, is having what Dewey would consider an "aesthetic experience." Driven by her perception of real-world exigencies and moral coherence, and guided by the tools (or skills) in her possession, Deming works through the media of writing and teaching to achieve beauty and meaning.

When Debbie tumbles head first off the cliff at Poamoho, Deming pragmatically saves her life . . . and takes in enough of the experience to appreciate the cosmological structure of the event—the possible roles of Christian faith, local deities, and chemical endorphins in saving the victim—and later develop an instructive narrative. Hers is an art of action combined with an art of ideas.

Alison Hawthorne Deming was born on July 13, 1946, in Hartford, Connecticut, two years after her brother, Rodney. Her mother, Travilla Bregny Macnab, from New York City, taught speech and dramatics part-time at the Ethel Walker School in the town of Simsbury, not far from the family's home in Avon. Deming's father, Benton Hawthorne Deming, a native of West Redding, Connecticut, worked in radio as a producer and announcer. Both parents were interested in literature and the performing arts. Her father acted in local theater productions and wrote stories, poems, and plays in his spare time, and her mother, too, wrote plays and directed productions at the local theater. They encouraged their children to be creative and to appreciate the arts. Alison grew up reading her parents' poems and plays. "That's brilliant, darling," they would tell her when she showed them her own efforts. Her parents also frequently sent her to the dictionary or thesaurus in pursuit of more interesting words, planting the seed for her continuing tendency to seek guidance in books. Not only has Alison made a life for herself in the literary arts, but her brother, now a construction supervisor in Los Angeles, continues to write screenplays on the side. When the children were growing up, the family lived in a home located on a woodsy knoll, overlooking Avon Mountain and the pastures of the Governor's Horse Guard. Her maternal grandmother, Marie Bregny Macnab, who lived with the Demings in the Avon house, was an important presence in the author's childhood.

Deming attended kindergarten in the one-room Pine Grove Schoolhouse in 1951. From 1952 to 1958, she went to Towpath Elementary School, often walking to the Avon Public Library after school. The library was the bookish child's favorite place, but she also enjoyed daily contact with nature in the then-rural town. Avon was growing, though, and Avon High School opened its doors in time for Alison to stay in town for high school. Earlier generations had been bused to neighboring Canton High School.

In 1954, one of the pivotal (and recurrent) experiences of Alison's life occurred when her family visited Grand Manan Island in New Brunswick, Canada, for two weeks in the summer. They stayed at Rose Cottage Inn, an old-fashioned family hotel. Her parents immediately fell in love with the island, and that summer, before leaving, they bought a house there, using a small inheritance Alison's mother had received from Frances Shedd, a librarian she had befriended in Wethersfield, Connecticut. Despite the complications that would eventually influence the course of her adult life, Deming has spent part of nearly every summer, from 1954 to the present, at Grand Manan, initially with her family and now sometimes alone. As her writing reveals, much of her thinking about the natural world has emerged from experiences on the island.

In the summer of 1963, Alison received a scholarship to attend the Transition-to-College Program at Hartford's Trinity College, where she encountered Latin poetry and comedy. Everything seemed to be on track for Alison's success in college. She graduated from Avon High School in 1964, and entered Pembroke College (the women's college associated with Brown University) in the fall. In November, though, she dropped out of college, pregnant, and married W. Scott Williams. Having considered such options as giving up her baby for adoption or having a risky, illegal abortion, she made a different choice. Her daughter, Lucinda Williams, was born in Hartford on March 21, 1965, and Alison gave up school, entered a forced marriage, and suffered emotional abandonment from her family because, as she explains today, "I had chosen my fate, and wanted to take responsibility for it."

In 1965, Deming moved to Cambridge, Massachusetts, with Lucinda and Scott. Her husband and her brother, Rodney, were students at Boston University. Alison was a full-time mom until, as she puts it, "things got rocky." Gradually, she began to be more independent, first making sandals and purses as a part-time leather shop employee, and then working in the slide collection at Harvard's Fogg Art Museum. Alison, Scott, and Rodney were all swept up in the sixties subculture, Scott and Rodney heavily into the drug scene, while Alison was more interested in the visions of cultural utopia that developed during that idealistic era. The marriage eventually frayed and came to an end. Alison had a few poet-friends from extension classes she was taking at Harvard. She enjoyed many pleasures of living in such a cultural center, attending modern dance classes and going to plays and museums. While living in Cambridge during the latter half of the 1960s, she began writing her own poetry, inspired by the literature she was reading—works by Sylvia Plath, Anne Sexton, Robert Lowell, Adrienne Rich, Denise Levertov, and others.

In the winter of 1969, Alison and Lucinda moved to Franklin County, Vermont. Alison wanted more autonomy as a mother and a place to raise Lucinda closer to nature and farther from the wounded culture that was reeling from the recent assassinations of John F. Kennedy, Bobby Kennedy, Martin Luther King Jr., and from the Vietnam War and the generational rift enflamed by counterculture ideals and accusations. Deming herself was still struggling with the emotional estrangement from her own parents caused by her early parenthood. Although at odds with her parents during these years, she was also deeply influenced by their pragmatic, self-sufficient approach to life. She made a living first as a dishwasher, then as a waitress, at a Vermont ski resort. Later, she started to teach at a "free school," helped to establish a parent cooperative elementary school, and eventually went to work as a paraprofessional outreach worker for a newly established family planning clinic, which had been created with the Johnson administration's War on Poverty funds. During these difficult years in Vermont, she was still writing poetry in her spare time, making friends with other poets, and reading the work of Gary Snyder, Wendell Berry, and Denise Levertov. As she discussed years later in her first book of essays and explained in a 1998 interview for the *Bloomsbury Review*, her father's notion of taking care of oneself had a lot to do with her own approach to survival:

> I wrote in *Temporary Homelands* that he would dig up his gardens by hand. Even in his 70s and

80s, he'd dig up a trench to replace a pipe, rather than calling someone else to do it. There was something about taking pride in having the strength to handle the discomforts and inconveniences, not being protected from that. A certain amount of hardship and discomfort is humbling. It teaches compassion for others. If we know no hardship, then it's difficult to imagine the hardship of others, to care for their misfortunes. During the years when I was poor with my daughter, I learned a lot about hardship, and it knocked a certain arrogance out of me that I had from growing up in a privileged situation. I'm grateful for that. I understood what it was to be poor.

Her effectiveness as a family planning educator led eventually to a position as county coordinator for Planned Parenthood of Vermont, a position she held from 1971 to 1974. She continued her public health work from 1975 to 1978 as director of the STD (Sexually Transmitted Disease) Control Program for the Vermont State Health Department. In addition to the public health teaching and administration, she worked at miscellaneous jobs throughout the 1970s, as a linotype operator, a farmhand on dairy and maple sugaring operations, and a sheep farmer. In 1979, Lucinda went off to prep school in New Hampshire and Alison moved to Portland, Maine, where she continued public health consulting intermittently until 1987 and began to devote increasing attention to her literary aspirations.

Having taken sporadic art and literature classes at the Harvard Extension Program, Deming shifted her attention to writing by connecting with "Firehouse" readings and the Poet's Mimeo Cooperative in Burlington, Vermont, from 1975 to 1979. She read poets from the Black Mountain School and encountered French surrealists, such as Apollinaire and Breton. The Burlington community gave her the opportunity to participate in study groups and writing workshops and led to early publications in the 1977 *Firehouse Anthology*. In 1978, her chapbook *Audel's Millwright's and Mechanic's Guide: A Re-Write* appeared from the Poet's Mimeo Cooperative. In 1980, having moved to Maine, she began to study for an M.F.A. in creative writing at Goddard College's low-residency program. Deming worked with Jack Myers, Roger Weingarten, Leslie Ullman, and Mark Doty, completing her degree in 1983, with an emphasis on poetry, after the M.F.A. program shifted to Vermont College. That year she began adjunct teaching at the University of Southern Maine, and her poem "Letter to Nathaniel Hawthorne" received the Pablo Neruda Prize from *Nimrod*, in a contest judged by Denise Levertov. The following year, she was awarded a fellowship at the Provincetown Fine Arts Work Center on Cape Cod, where she was influenced by Stanley Kunitz, Alan Dugan, and Mary Oliver, and earned additional income by reading to painter Myron Stout after he became blind. From 1987 to 1988, she held a Wallace Stegner Fellowship in Poetry at Stanford University, an opportunity to refine her craft under the tutelage of Levertov, Kenneth Fields, and W. S. Di Piero.

After her year at Stanford, Deming returned to Provincetown, Massachusetts, to work as the Writing Program Coordinator from 1988 to 1990 at the Fine Arts Work Center. In 1990, she was named director of the Poetry Center at the University of Arizona, a position she held until 2000, when she moved full-time into her teaching position as a tenured, associate professor of creative writing at the university. Counting her work for Planned Parenthood and State of Vermont's STD Control Program in the 1970s, as well as her work as an arts administrator in the 1980s and 1990s, Deming spent nearly thirty years in administration while developing her skills and credentials as a poet and essayist, keeping one foot in the practical realm of budgets and schedules and the other in the realm of words and images. Her high-profile supervisory work has included a position as vice president of the Associated Writing Programs from 1995 to 1999, and her current service on the Orion Society's board of directors. During the 1990s, with the aid of two, year-long poetry fellowships from the National Endowment for the Arts (1990 and 1995) and residencies at such artist colonies as the Djerassi Foundation in California, the Island Institute in Alaska, and Yaddo in upstate New York, she began to publish a series of highly regarded books of poetry and nonfiction, most recently a limited edition chapbook called *Anatomy of Desire: The Daughter/Mother Sessions* with Lucinda Bliss, published by Tucson's Kore Press in 2000 in conjunction with an exhibit of Lucinda's paintings at the University of Arizona's art gallery.

In addition to its pragmatism, its "integrative aesthetic" (as philosopher John Dewey might call it) that pulls together ethics, worldly action, and formal integrity, the recurrent, singular features of Alison Deming's work are the emphasis on *place* in general (or on particular places that are important in her life) and the writer's abiding fascination with natural science. Place and nature are prominent themes in her five books to date: two poetry collections, two books of essays, and an edited anthology. Deming's first book of poetry, *Science and Other Poems,* appeared in 1994. This volume, like her first book of essays, *Temporary Homelands,* which came out the same year, foregrounds places she has lived or visited, the processes and ethical aspects of science and art, and points of intersection between the human self and the more-than-human world. For example, the poem "Mt. Lemmon, Steward Observatory, 1990" contemplates the limitations of lavishly funded science, the fact that even the most fabulous new telescope cannot make the mysteries of nature fully accessible to our understanding. What we really need, she implies in the opening stanza, is simply direct contact:

> What it takes to dazzle us, masters of dazzle,
> all of us here together at the top of the world,
> is a night without neon or mercury lamps.
> Black sheen flowing above,

the stars, unnamed and disorderly—
diamonds, a ruby or sapphire,
scattered and made
more precious for being cut
from whatever strand
once held them together.
The universe is emptiness and dust,
occasional collisions, collapsing zones of gas,
electrical bursts, and us.

The most startling revelation, once artificial lights and machinery have been stripped away, is that we are part of the universe, connected to the distant forces and phenomena that so compel our attention. Other poems in the collection, such as "The Man Who Became a Deer," dedicated to Alaska nature writer Richard Nelson, extend this theme of attachment to nature, as when she writes:

The muscle, the blood,
the hair and the skin
replaced themselves
cell by cell—each one
incorporating the molecules
of deer which he ate
three times a day. And
the deer remained hidden,
disguised as a man
in the perfect camouflage
of his body. Sometimes
in his face his friends
would see a quickness,

in his legs a jitter,
a tensing to leap—
his patience became that
of a browser, his heart
that of a hart, and his brain
which only loses, day after day,
never gains cells, woke up
one winter morning to
the heat of the blood of deer
running through its
pipes like antifreeze.

Encounters with places and equivocations about the goals and possibilities of science, combined with reflections on the strains and satisfactions of tradition, appear throughout *Science and Other Poems*. "One inherits too much baggage to ever / step clear of the past," she writes in "Letter to Nathaniel Hawthorne," a lengthy poem that explores the life of her great-great-grandfather and attempts to plumb his literary compulsion, as if blaming him for her own persistent need to craft and create. At the same time, her parental musings in "Snapshots for My Daughter" suggest her own complicity in generational trauma: "I gave you what you needed but I couldn't / make it easy. That night I dreamed / I carried a baby so small / the birth was painless, but the deeper rip / where the blood-lace last connected us / ached a long while into morning." Amid the more fretful and serious poems, such as "Grand Manan" and "Searching for the Lost," there are playful lyrics about her intractable identity, represented by such things as the unmanageability of hair: "I think Heraclitus should have used hair / instead of the river," she jokes in "At the Hairdresser's I Think of Heraclitus," "each cell a tiny model of the soul / growing by the logos of its need / so that the hairdresser / never cuts the same hair twice."

Temporary Homelands: Essays on Nature, Spirit, and Place, also from 1994, is divided into four sections, emphasizing experiences at Grand Manan, meditations on American culture and family tradition, efforts to root herself in the American West upon moving to Tucson in 1990, and new thoughts about art and science inspired, in part, by experiences in Alaska. "I wanted to write an honest book about my relationship with nature," she writes in the preface,

> not to offer theories or prescriptions for what that relationship ought to be. I wanted to examine how I actually experience nature, not by defining it, but by engaging with it as an ongoing process of encounter and by making it show itself as a process rooted in family and cultural history. I wanted to understand the places, events, and ideas in my own experience that seem most significant in shaping that relationship, and to explore the quality of reflection that certain loved places seem to induce. This book, finally, is about one thing—reconstructing an intimacy with nature. We live in a time of radical loss—loss of space, places, tribes, and species. Loss of a sense of belonging in and to a place. Loss of continuity and coherence. We

live with a painful sense that the human species is the most destructive force on the planet. Even so, the fact ironically remains that we are embedded in nature. Every second of every day we are in relationship with that force—it is what we are.

In essay after essay, Deming explores the possibility of continued (or renewed) intimacy with nature, even in this era of diminishment and increasing technological interference. She demonstrates the de lights of being an attentive amateur naturalist, the surprise and stimulation of moving to (or visiting) new landscapes, and the complementary perspectives of science and art.

One of the most compelling and liberating passages in the book occurs in the final essay of the collection, which recounts the author's experience working in a clinic for injured raptors while doing a residency at the Island Institute in Sitka, Alaska, in 1992. She mentions her initial insecurity as a student of nature, tentative about the possible role of art in the age of formal science:

> Living in the age of experts often makes me fearful that I don't know enough to know what I am seeing. I have been working on eagles for two weeks. More and more I feel that, in the Indian way, the eagles are working on me. What I want to know can be learned with eyes, ears, patience, binoculars, and a library card. Not for me the heroics of the federal biologist flying

across the polar icecap with a bush pilot, down-ing a polar bear with tranquilizer darts, tattoo-ing the paws, and pulling out a molar to find out how old the creature is. Just by sitting in the right place with my eyes opened I can watch a star-mass of eagles whirling hundreds of feet in the air. Each time I try to box off a section of blue sky, to be more scientific and count the gliders, I see that farther up more eagles are soaring, and more beyond them—dark specks barely moving against the high, fair weather clouds. I count twenty—forty—but it's useless to try. The smaller and smaller they get, the more the sky looks like it's eagles all the way up.

Even in expressing the literary naturalist's feeling of insecurity, if not inferiority, as a student of nature, the writer displays profound ability to represent the natural phenomenon she's observing and to evoke the feeling of this experience, the sense of wonder and aesthetic rapture. The result, in the paragraph that follows, is a paean to the magnificent flight of eagles:

Two of the star-mass glide into synchrony hun-dreds of feet in the air. Wing tips glance, one twirls beneath the other in a half cartwheel, talons up, nearly grasping the talons reaching down from the eagle above it, then flipping upright to soar by its companion's side. This courting goes on for hours—two eagles circling in the abundance of one another's energy, one

tumbling underneath, then cartwheeling back
into upright flight. I am eager to see for myself
the behavior I've read about—the two birds
locking talons and falling into a whirling dive,
first one then the other tumbling upside down
in a kind of trust dance bringing them nearly to
the ground. I see only this repeated approach
and retreat, an intense mutuality taking place
in the sky. A king salmon leaps out of the water,
the full length of its body arcing through the
air, back-fin taut and translucent in the sun.
The eagles don't bother to descend, more interested, for the moment, in entertaining a hunger
for each other.

Eyes, ears, patience, binoculars, and a library card—
combined with the poet's flair and the essayist's gift
for explanation—result in this memorable passage,
the culminating statement of *Temporary Homelands*.

In 1996, Deming asserted herself as an arbiter
and supporter of literary culture in the western states
by producing *Poetry of the American West: A Columbia
Anthology*, seeking to offer a collection that spans the
variety of geographical and cultural perspectives that
constitute the West, ranging from the one hundredth
meridian to the Pacific Coast and from the Canadian
border to the Mexican border (with the exception of
Nahuatl flower songs from Mexico, which she chooses
to include). "For the scrupulous contemporary observer," she writes in the preface, "no American landscape can be seen without also seeing the history of

people's relationship with the land and with one another." Poetry becomes the lens for understanding space, aridity, and the collisions and intersections of cultures that mark the West. This anthology implies the editor's at-homeness in the American Southwest, despite her upbringing as a New Englander bearing the famous Hawthorne name and the cultural and psychological baggage implied by her roots.

If the first book of essays emphasizes (in its title and in the itinerant foci of many individual essays) the ideas of passage, movement, and temporariness, Deming's next book, *The Monarchs: A Poem Sequence,* published in 1997, is a prolonged series of meditations (sixty poems in all) on the intelligence that enables monarch butterflies—and humans—to navigate the terrain of space and relationships. The opening poem reveals the trope of comparing butterfly migration and the real and metaphorical journeys of modern human lives:

> Their navigation takes science—an animated
> scrap of paper flying two thousand miles
> for the first time each year (a nine-month
> life) and making it. And art to know
> to move when the idea strikes. Idea?
> A butterfly idea? What could be smaller
> or more frantic—yet correct. The beauties
> survive.
>
> I like to think the same intelligence,
> whatever makes the monarchs fly,
> is at work in my friends who shed

jobs and marriages the way a eucalyptus
ruptures out of its bark as it grows.

In a manner reminiscent of Robert Duncan's well-
known poem sequence called "Passages," Deming in-
cludes an intermittent sequence, a numbered series
entitled "Essay on Intelligence," within the monarch
meditations. The resulting pattern suggests the recur-
rence of a suborder within the larger collection of
linked human-butterfly analogies, speculations about
the science of butterfly navigation ("Given, a speck
of magnetite / (ferrous oxide) is / lodged in a butterfly's / head, yet how does metal / tell the nerves, /
turn here, lift, take on / water for ballast, as the /
monarch must do—not a / powerful flier, subject / to
wing wear and drift— / in finding its winter groves?"),
and critiques of the human practices that threaten
to destroy butterfly populations. The sequence as a
whole is a tour de force of lyricism, knowledge, and
conscience—a major literary achievement and a land-
mark in late-twentieth-century American environmental literature.

In her interview with Jihyuk Han for the
Bloomsbury Review shortly after the publication of
The Monarchs, Deming reflected on the importance
of the phenomenon of "place" in her writing:

It's significant both in the poetry and prose. I
write about experiences that seem intense or
that seem to jazz my mental energy up. Often
when I go to a place that's unfamiliar to me, I
have this enlivened experience, and there's the

113 ✐

delightful delusion that I'm the first person to perceive this. I don't have all the layers of experiencing the place, and so I feel I've just arrived from a foreign planet. I have a very poor memory, so I write things down, because I don't want to lose the richness of that experience. It's partly that place is something that happens in my perception; it's not a decision that I made to write about place, but place makes me feel more curious about the world. I think it also has to do with the fact that the human population is expanding so quickly, and we're losing so many places. There are many places in my life that have been important that I can't go back to, because they are gone now. Where there was a farm, there's now a shopping mall. Where there was a friendly village, there's now a city. The sense of loss is profound. I have the feeling that if I write this, I will always be able to know and remember this place, as I'm experiencing it now. It's a way of holding onto things that are just painfully evanescent.

In *The Edges of the Civilized World: A Journey in Nature and Culture,* her second collection of essays, published in 1998, Deming builds on the realization Bill McKibben and others have articulated in recent decades that "change [is] happening nearly everywhere during this age when humanity sprawls across the world, ever eager for new experience and opportunity, ever ready to turn a new limitation into some kind of growth." Supported by an NEA grant, she traveled to tranquil Pacific City on the Oregon coast to reflect for a year on a "constellation" of troubling questions that resulted from her experiences in various places, from Baja California to Hawai'i:

> What is civilization? Where and how is it being formed? On what assumptions is it founded? What should we hope for the future of humanity and our world? To what extent can our ideas, hopes, and will shape the future? What has civilization blurred and rejected that we might clarify and call back into our shepherding intelligence? What lessons did our ancestors learn that we should not forget? And what of their practices would we be better off leaving behind? It is the late twentieth century, and one can do nothing without doubts and questions.

The eleven essays collected in *Edges* extend stories and meditations begun in *Temporary Homelands*, intensifying chronic worries with a millennialist angst. The opening essay, "The Value of Experience," echoes the title of Robert Michael Pyle's well-known essay, "The Extinction of Experience," but gives the topic a somewhat more optimistic twist, explaining the value—for her—of traveling to places in the world "where people still live in primary relationship with nature." Feeling alienated from her "self-devouring culture," she yearns to "leave again, searching for evidence of another way of existence, for a new experience that will make the world real again." The essay implies the possibility, even today, of finding examples of this other "way of existence." The final piece in the book, "The Islands," concludes by depicting the formation of the earth's newest land, where lava spills from a volcano into the Pacific, cooling into rock as it hits the water—an image of renewal and optimism, following a series of essays about the steady encroachment of possible and actual destruction throughout the world, the spread of what we call "civilization." The essay "Poetry and Science: A View from the Divide" attempts to heal the classic rift between the "two cultures," arguing that the reform of civilization requires cooperation among physicists and poets. To those (poets among them) who would argue that science is the source of many of our present worries, she asserts, "What science-bashers fail to appreciate is that scientists, in their unflagging attraction to the unknown, *love* what they don't know. It guides and motivates their work; it keeps them up late at night; and it makes that work poetic." One cannot read Alison Deming's work, either the poetry or the essays, without recognizing the seriousness of the world's current dilemmas, the continued beauty of the changing planet, and the hope inherent to contemporary environmental literature's stories of sadness, perplexity, and love.

Deming's current projects extend the earlier work in surprising new directions. After spending part of the summer of 1999 teaching in the Prague Summer Seminars, she became fascinated with the human legacy of high culture and high horror that have been intertwined in European history. The poetry manuscript she is now finishing, titled *Genius Loci* (from the ten-page title poem), considers beauty and horror in the context of geography, building upon her abiding interest in place. As this *Credo* essay goes to press, Deming is also collaborating with geologist Lauret Savoy to edit an anthology called *The Colors of Nature: A Multicultural Anthology,* a book that aims to broaden the traditional, Eurocentric definition of "nature writing" by offering fifteen to twenty essays (primarily new work) by African-American, Latino, Asian-American, Native, and mixed-blood writers.

When I feel disheartened about the condition of the planet, I turn for encouragement to the inspiring example of Alison Deming's life and work, and that of her close colleagues, such as Gary Paul Nabhan and Scott Russell Sanders, in the tight-knit community of contemporary American nature writers. Two snapshots come to mind. The anthropologist Terre Sattefield and I traveled to Tucson in April of 1998 to interview Deming and several other writers about the intersections between storytelling and environmental values. Following the conversations, Terre had to fly home to British Columbia, but I stayed for an extra day to hike with Alison on the King Canyon Trail west of Tucson. It had been a wet spring, and the desert was flaring with color, from the pink blossoms of prickly pear to assorted yellows and oranges of desert flowers. I have two favorite photographs from that morning walk: one of Alison, the transplanted

New Englander, pretending to hug a saguaro cactus; the other, taken from the side, as she handles and inspects the wing of a small bird, the rest of which has vanished, presumably consumed by a predator. These are images of curiosity and the sense of being at home. Alison Hawthorne Deming, still in the energetic prime of her writing career, has followed an unconventional path to her current place in the world—a path fraught with trauma and hardship, surmounted by way of persistence, imagination, and a pragmatic knack for solving problems. Some of the clues to her worldview are offered in this *Credo* essay.

Bibliography of Alison Hawthorne Deming's Work

by Scott Slovic

BOOKS

The Edges of the Civilized World. New York:
St. Martin's/Picador USA, 1998.

The Monarchs: A Poem Sequence. Baton Rouge:
Louisiana State University Press, 1997.

Science and Other Poems. Baton Rouge: Louisiana
State University Press, 1994.

Temporary Homelands. San Francisco: Mercury House,
1994 (cloth edition). *Temporary Homelands:
Essays on Nature, Spirit, and Place*. New York: St.
Martin's/Picador USA, 1996 (paperback edition).

EDITED BOOKS

Poetry of the American West: A Columbia Anthology.
New York: Columbia University Press, 1996 (cloth
edition). New York: Columbia University Press,
1999 (paperback edition).

CHAPBOOKS

With Lucinda Bliss. *Anatomy of Desire: The Daughter/Mother Sessions.* Tucson: Kore Press, 2000.

Girls in the Jungle: What Does It Take for a Woman to Survive in the Arts? Tucson: Kore Press, 1995.

Audel's Millwright's and Mechanic's Guide: A Re-Write. Burlington, Vt.: Poet's Mimeo Cooperative, 1978.

UNCOLLECTED JOURNAL AND MAGAZINE PUBLICATIONS—POEMS

"Things to Do around Grand Manan." *Writing Nature* (Summer 1999): 14.

"Arboretum," "La Paz," "Animats," and "Ordinary Air." *Hawai'i Review* 21.2, no. 50 (Summer 1998): 171–76.

"The Naturalists" and "Wild Fruit." *Alaska Quarterly Review* 16, nos. 3–4 (Spring/Summer 1998): 150–54.

"The List" and "Making Love to You When You're Far Away." *Hayden's Ferry Review,* no. 19 (Fall/Winter 1996): 92–95.

"Learning Again to Love" and "Yosemite Notebook." *Nebraska Review* 24, no. 1 (Fall/Winter 1996): 65–67.

"Anemones," "The Earth," "Blewit, Repandum, Agaricus," "The Phenomenology of Shopping," and "In Spring: Drift Creek." *Wild Duck Review* 2, no. 4 (June/July 1996): 19.

"The Rock Fig," "The Gulf," and "Driving through

Nature." *Southwestern American Literature* 21, no. 1 (Fall 1995): 136–40.

"The Magi." *Equinox: Writing for a New Culture* 11, no. 1 (Fall 1993): 9.

"For the Girls." *Shankpainter* (Winter 1985): 35–36.

"The Telescope" and "The Purpose of Fear." *Great River Review* 5, no. 2 (Summer 1984): 119–20, 230.

"Lady Godiva." *Calliope* 7, no. 2 (May 1984): 23–27.

"Sex Life of the Cardinal." *Kennebec* 8 (Spring 1984): 7.

"Sculptor." *Portland Review of the Arts,* no. 4 (Spring 1984): 76.

"On Meeting House Hill." *Morning Sentinel* (April 1982): 5.

"Experience" and "This Is for You." *Portland Review of the Arts* 2, no. 1 (April 1982): 55.

"Neighbors Once Lovers" and "The House with Aluminum Siding." *Louisville Review,* no. 12 (Spring 1982): 24–25.

"Lunch outside the Aquarium." *Morning Sentinel* (December 1981): 5.

"Dropping into Sleep." *Morning Sentinel* (September 1981): 5.

"Decoration Day." *Maine Times* (July 1981).

"Patriots' Day at the Baker's Table." *Kennebec* (Spring 1981): 10.

"Light Birds on a Red Brick Wall." *Firehouse* 25 (January 1981).

"A Man in Tucson." *Penumbra* 2, no. 2 (3rd/4th quarter 1980): 3.

"Abattoir Sequence." *Firehouse* 23 (October 1978).

"Virgins, Grandmothers and a Japanese Print." *Firehouse* 19 (November 1977).

"Correspondence with Saint Valentine." *Firehouse* 14 (April 1977).

"The Myth of Fame" and "Postcards from Grand Manan." *Firehouse* 12 (October 1976).

"Stirring Up Voices." *New Letters* (Summer 1976): 30–31.

"Disheveled," "September 15, 1975," and "The Force That Moves." *Firehouse* 6 (January 1976).

"Bucolics." *News and the Weather* (Summer 1975): 13.

UNCOLLECTED JOURNAL AND MAGAZINE PUBLICATIONS—ESSAYS

"Beach Watching on Two Islands." *Islands* 20, no. 8 (December 2000) 90–101.

"Crossing Borders with Homero Aridjis." *Orion Afield* (Summer 2000): 42–43.

"The Practical Poet." *Poets and Writers* (April 1999): 76–80.

"Sacred Hawai'i." *Islands* 19, no. 2 (March/April 1999): 86–97.

"Remembering Manoa." *You Are Here: The Journal of Creative Geography* 1, no. 1 (Spring/Summer 1998): 13.

"Judge's Legacy of Pain." *Denver Post* (December 29, 1996): 1D–5D.

With Richard Nelson and Scott Russell Sanders. "A Call to Action." *Orion* 14, no. 4 (Autumn 1995): 5.

"Poetry and the World Household." *Hayden's Ferry Review,* no. 12 (Spring/Summer 1993): 75–79.

"The Light Switch in the Dark." *Shankpainter* (Spring 1992): 1–4.

ANTHOLOGY APPEARANCES

"The Rock Fig" and "Driving through Nature." In *Getting Over the Color Green: Contemporary Southwestern Environmental Literature,* edited by Scott Slovic. Tucson: University of Arizona Press, 2001.

"The Practice of Humanity." In *Learning to Glow: A Nuclear Reader,* edited by John Bradley. Tucson: University of Arizona Press, 2000.

"Tilden Park." In *Urban Nature: Poems about Wildlife in the City,* edited by Laure-Anne Bosselaar. Minneapolis: Milkweed Editions, 2000.

"Science and Poetry: A View from the Divide." In *A View from the Divide: Creative Nonfiction on Health and Science,* edited by Lee Gutkind. Pittsburgh: University of Pittsburgh Press, 1999.

"Science" and "The Monarchs, 18." In *The Yellow Shoe Poets,* edited by George Garrett. Baton Rouge: Louisiana State University Press, 1999.

"Science," "Mt. Lemmon," "Observatory, 1990," "The Woman Painting Crates," and "The Monarchs, 17, 24, 26, 28, 38, 40, 46, 52." In *Verse and Universe: Poems about Science and Mathematics,* edited by Kurt Brown. Minneapolis: Milkweed Editions, 1998.

"Sanctuary." In *Wild Song: Poems of the Natural World,*
edited by John Daniel. Athens: University of
Georgia Press, 1998.

"The Monarchs, 3, 22, 23, 25, 34." In *Fever Dreams:
Contemporary Arizona Poetry,* edited by Leilani
Wright and James Cervantes. Tucson: University
of Arizona Press, 1997.

"Caffe Trieste" and "Saturday, J.'s Oyster Bar." In
*Night Out: Poems about Hotels, Motels, Restaurants,
and Bars,* edited by Kurt Brown and Laure-Anne
Bosselaar. Minneapolis: Milkweed Editions, 1997.

"The Man Who Became a Deer" and "The Woman
Painting Crates." In *Discovering Literature: Stories,
Poems, Plays,* edited by Hans P. Guth and Gabriele
L. Rico. New York: Prentice-Hall, 1996.

"Claiming the Yard." In *The Earth at Our Doorstep,*
edited by Annie Stine. San Francisco: Sierra Club
Books, 1996.

"How We Did It." In *Homemaking: Women Writers
and the Politics and Poetics of Home,* edited by
C. Wiley and F. R. Barnes. New York: Garland
Publishing, 1996.

"Science." In *Sixty Years of American Poetry,* edited
by the Academy of American Poets. New York:
Harry N. Abrams, 1996.

"Woods Work." In *American Nature Writing: A Sierra
Club Annual,* edited by John Murray. San Francisco:
Sierra Club Books, 1995.

"The Nature of Poetry: Poetry in Nature." In *Writing
It Down for James: Writers on Life and Craft,* vol. 2,
edited by Kurt Brown. Boston: Beacon Press, 1995.

"Caffe Trieste." In *Cape Discovery: The Fine Arts Work Center Anthology,* edited by Bruce Smith and Catherine Gannon. Riverdale-on-Hudson, N.Y.: Sheepmeadow Press, 1994.

"The Monarchs, 1–8." In *Place of the Wild: A Wildlands Anthology,* edited by David Clarke Burks. Washington, D.C.: Island Press, 1994.

"An Island Notebook." In *The Pushcart Prize XVIII: Best of the Small Presses,* edited by Bill Henderson. Wainscott, N.Y.: Pushcart Press, 1993.

"Canoeing the Salt Marsh" and "Dreamwork with Horses." In *The Forgotten Language: Contemporary Poets and Nature,* edited by Christopher Merrill. Salt Lake City: Peregrine Smith, 1991.

"Canoeing the Salt Marsh," "The Monarchs, 1–4," "The Russians," and "Saturday, J.'s Oyster Bar." In *The Eloquent Edge: Fifteen Maine Women Writers,* edited by Kathleen Lignell. Bar Harbor, Maine: Acadia Press, 1990.

"Science" and "My Intention." In *The Uncommon Touch: Poetry and Fiction from the Stanford Writing Program,* edited by John L'Heureux. Stanford: Stanford University, 1989.

"Meteor Invocation," "Portrait of a Neighbor," "Winter at the Farm," "A Memorial for Suzanne," "Two Men at the Bar," "Three Images of Love," "Heroes and Heroines," and "Again, the Heart." In *Firehouse Anthology,* edited by Tinker Green, Alison Hawthorne Deming, Bill Davis, Michael Breiner, and Arthur Stone. Burlington, Vt.: Poet's Mimeo Cooperative, 1977.

"Sequences," "Marriage," and "Life on the Island."
In *Country Women's Anthology,* edited by Christina
Huff, Jennifer Johnson, and Marnie Purple. Albion,
Calif.: Country Women Publication, 1976.

SOUND RECORDINGS

The Monarchs: A Poem Sequence. Read by the author.
Kore Press, January 2000.
Reading from *The Monarchs* by Garrison Keillor on
The Writer's Almanac, Minnesota Public Radio,
August 8, 1999, and September 27, 1999.
"Alison Hawthorne Deming." A reading. University
of Arizona Poetry Center, November 4, 1998.
"Light Birds on a Red Brick Wall." Read by the
author with jazz musicians Roy Frazee and Joe
LaFlamme. Produced by *Interlude Magazine.*
Portland, Maine, November 1982.

VIDEO RECORDINGS

"Alison Hawthorne Deming: *The Monarchs.*" *Books
and Company,* program #606. KAET-TV, Tempe,
Arizona, April 1998.
"Alison Hawthorne Deming." A reading. San
Francisco State University Poetry Center Archives,
March 17, 1994.

INTERVIEWS

Engley, Hollis. "From Orcas to Martha's Vineyard:
Places Apart." *Seattle Times* (August 21, 1994).

———. "Islands Lure Presidents and Vacation Purists." *Boston Herald* (August 2, 1994).

Froyd, Susan. "Wild in the Streets." *Westword* (October 14, 1999): 36.

Han, Jihyuk. "The Poetry of Place: An Interview with Alison Hawthorne Deming." *Bloomsbury Review* 8, no. 2 (March/April 1998): 7–8.

Kocher, Ruth Ellen. "A Question of Survival: An Interview with Alison Hawthorne Deming." *Hayden's Ferry Review,* no. 14 (Spring/Summer 1994): 75–92.

Porter, William. "Well Versed in Hospitality: UA Poetry Center Offers Literary Oasis." *Arizona Republic* (January 16, 1997).

Regan, Margaret. "Deming on Deming." *Tucson Weekly* (September 7, 1994).

BIOGRAPHICAL/CRITICAL STUDIES AND REVIEWS

Armstrong, Gene. "New Muse Settles In." *Arizona Daily Star* (September 30, 1990).

Balzar, John. "Wide Open Spaces." *Los Angeles Times Book Review* (December 8, 1996): 5.

Becker, Robin. "The Personal Is Political Is Postmodern." *American Poetry Review* 23, no. 6 (November/December 1994): 23–26.

Budin, Sue E. Review of *Science and Other Poems.* *Kliatt* (November 1994): 26.

Bugeja, Michael J. "Accessible to All." *Writer's Digest* 78, no. 10 (October 1998): 12–15.

———. Review of *Science and Other Poems*. *Cream City Review* 18, no. 2 (1994): 272–75.

Chappell, Fred. "'A Million Million Suns': Poetry and Science." *Georgia Review* 49, no. 3 (Fall 1995): 711–26.

Chuang, Angie. "Verses of Diversity." *Arizona Republic* (August 30, 1994).

Dagnal-Myron, Cynthia M. "Poet's Solace Is Lingual Music." *Arizona Daily Star* (April 2, 1995).

DeNicola, Deborah. "The Idea of Order." *Boston Book Review* 1, no. 4 (Fall 1994).

English, Susan. "Finding a Place: A Fresh Voice in Nature Writing, Deming Makes Fluent Transition from Poetry to Essay Form." *Spokesman Review* (October 2, 1994).

Friedman, Paula. "Land and Loss: A Sustaining Wilderness." *San Francisco Review* 21, no. 6 (November/December 1996): 31.

Gates, Michelle. "Poetry Connects Science and Spirit." *CSU Collegian* (October 14, 1996).

Gillen, Katherine E. Review of *Temporary Homelands*. *Kliatt* (January 1997): 27.

Gioia, Dana. Review of *Science and Other Poems*. *Washington Post* (December 4, 1994): 12.

Griego, Francis S. Review of *Temporary Homelands*. *Electronic Green Journal* 2, no. 2 (December 1995).

Heller, Amanda. Review of *The Edges of the Civilized World*. *Boston Globe* (December 13, 1998): M2.

Hubbuch, C. K. Review of *Science and Other Poems*. *Hungry Mind Review,* no. 46 (Summer 1998): 41.

Jordan, Teresa. "Making the Future Possible." Review

of *Poetry of the American West*. *Bloomsbury Review* 16, no. 4 (July/August 1996): 13.

Lowe, Charlotte. "Reaping Rewards of Poetry." *Tucson Citizen* (September 8, 1994).

Lucas, John. Review of *Science and Other Poems*. *Stand Magazine* 36 (Summer 1995): 81.

Martin, J. C. Review of *Poetry of the American West*. *Arizona Daily Star* (April 7, 1996).

Moeckel, Nancy. Review of *Temporary Homelands*. *Library Journal* 119, no. 13 (August 1994): 110.

Monaghan, Pat. Review of *Science and Other Poems*. *Booklist* 90, no. 15 (April 1, 1994): 1419.

Mushkatel, Jessica and Adam Georgandis. "Poetry Center Director Enlarging Accessibility." *Arizona Daily Wildcat* (September 13, 1990).

Niemi, Judith. "Tourist Traps." Review of *The Edges of the Civilized World*. *Women's Review of Books* 16, no. 6 (March 1999): 13–14.

Painter, Nannette. Review of *The Monarchs*. utah.citysearch.com (May 1999).

Porter, William. "Land Out West Lures Poets' Best." *Albuquerque Tribune* (June 28, 1996).

———. "Writing the Range: Through Centuries of Poetry, the West Finds Its Voice." *Arizona Republic* (April 28, 1996).

Rawlins, C. L. Review of *The Monarchs*. *Stonecrop* (Winter 1997): 56.

Review of *The Edges of the Civilized World*. *Santa Fe New Mexican* (May 30, 1999).

Review of *The Edges of the Civilized World*. *Orion* 18, no. 2 (Spring 1999): 70.

Review of *The Edges of the Civilized World. Arizona Daily Star* (December 6, 1998).

Review of *The Edges of the Civilized World. Publishers Weekly* 245, no. 41 (October 12, 1998): 67.

Review of *The Edges of the Civilized World. Kirkus Reviews* 66, no. 23 (October 1, 1998): 1425.

Review of *The Monarchs. American Poet* (Spring 1998).

Review of *The Monarchs. Maine Sunday Telegram* (January 11, 1998).

Review of *Poetry of the American West. San Jose Mercury News* (December 15, 1996).

Review of *Poetry of the American West. Eugene Register-Guard* (September 22, 1996).

Review of *Poetry of the American West. Westways Magazine* (September 1996).

Review of *Poetry of the American West. Valley Magazine* (September 1996).

Review of *Poetry of the American West. Rocky Mountain News* (August 25, 1996).

Review of *Poetry of the American West. Omaha World-Herald* (August 12, 1996).

Review of *Poetry of the American West. Albuquerque Monthly* (August 1996): 9.

Review of *Poetry of the American West. Chico News and Review* (July 18, 1996).

Review of *Poetry of the American West. Midwest Book Review* (June/July 1996).

Review of *Poetry of the American West. Houston Tribune* (June 1996).

Review of *Poetry of the American West. Times and Post-Intelligencer* (May 19, 1996).

Review of *Poetry of the American West. Publishers Weekly* 243, no. 3 (January 15, 1996): 374.

Review of *Temporary Homelands. Common Boundary* (January/February 1995).

Review of *Temporary Homelands. NAPRA Trade Journal* (Holiday 1994).

Review of *Temporary Homelands. Feminist Bookstore News* 17, no. 4 (November/December 1994): 85.

Review of *Temporary Homelands. New Age Retailer* (October 1994).

Review of *Temporary Homelands. San Francisco Focus* (August 1994).

Review of *Temporary Homelands. Los Angeles Times Book Review* (July 31, 1994): 6.

Review of *Temporary Homelands. Publishers Weekly* 241, no. 26 (June 27, 1994): 65.

Review of *Temporary Homelands. Kirkus Reviews* 62, no. 11 (June 1, 1994): 750.

Review of *Science and Other Poems. Publishers Weekly* 241, no. 17 (April 25, 1994): 66.

Review of *Temporary Homelands. Values and Visions* 25, no. 4 (1994).

Robbins, Kenneth. "The Nature of Nature Writing." Review of *Temporary Homelands. Bloomsbury Review* 15, no. 4 (July/August 1995): 25.

Scheper, Dianne Ganz. "Our Erotic Center." Review of *Temporary Homelands. Belles Lettres* 10, no. 2 (Spring 1995): 32–33.

Seaman, Donna. Review of *Temporary Homelands. Booklist* 90, no. 22 (August 1994): 1419.

———. Review of *The Edges of the Civilized World*. *Booklist* 95, no. 4 (October 15, 1998): 375.

Simon, Maurya. "Finding Ourselves in the Difficult World." *Journal* (Fall/Winter 1995).

Slavick, Allison. Review of *The Edges of the Civilized World*. *Rain Taxi* 4, no. 1 (Spring 1999): 37.

St. Germaine, Dennis. "Science and Poetry." *Report on Research* 10, no. 1 (Fall/Winter 1993–1994).

Stromenger, Lela. "People Not Interlopers in Poet's Wilderness." *Arizona Republic* (October 23, 1994).

"The Best Poetry." *Bloomsbury Review* 15, no. 1 (January/February 1995).

Thorpe, Peter. Review of *Science and Other Poems*. *Bloomsbury Review* 15, no. 2 (March/April 1995): 21.

Westra, Brian. Review of *The Edges of the Civilized World*. *Library Journal* 124, no. 1 (January 1999): 143.

Wolf, Edward C. "'Homelands' Explores Relationships with Nature." *Seattle Times Book Review* (September 18, 1994).

Wunderlich, Mark. Review of *Poetry of the American West*. *Boston Review* 22, no. 1 (February/March 1997): 46.

ACKNOWLEDGMENTS FOR "WRITING THE SACRED INTO THE REAL"

by Alison Hawthorne Deming

The title of this *Credo* is derived from a comment made by poet Eleanor Wilner in a talk she gave in February 1998 at the University of Arizona Poetry Center. My best recollection of her statement is, "Our task is to get the sacred back into the real." My gratitude to her for this wisdom and many others that live in her poems. I have been blessed by the nourishment of several communities of writers, each of which has provided friendships that challenged and sustained me: the Poet's Mimeo Cooperative in Burlington, Vermont; the low-residency M.F.A. Program at Vermont College; the Fine Arts Work Center in Provincetown, Massachusetts; the Wallace Stegner Fellowship Program at Stanford University; the University of Arizona Poetry Center; and the Orion Society.

Once again, my thanks go to the *Georgia Review,*

which published the third section of this essay in their Summer 2000 issue. Stephen Corey's close editorial eye consistently makes me pay attention to what I have missed, and I am grateful to him for making me more lucid than I would otherwise appear to be.

Finally, my gratitude goes to my mother, Travilla Deming, who taught me perseverance and the love of language.

WORKS CITED

p. ix   Mircea Eliade, *The Sacred and the Profane* (New York: Harcourt, Brace and Company, 1987), 116–17.

p. ix   Walt Whitman, *Leaves of Grass* (New York: Modern Library, 1944), 63.

p. 5   Octavio Paz, *The Double Flame* (New York: Harcourt, Brace and Company, 1995), 274.

p. 12   T. S. Eliot, "Shakespeare and the Stoicism of Seneca," in *Selected Essays* (New York: Harcourt, Brace and Company, 1950), 117.

p. 21   William Kittredge, *Who Owns the West?* (San Francisco: Mercury House, 1996), 158–59.

p. 32   Paz, *The Double Flame,* 274.

p. 35   Ralph Waldo Emerson, "The Transcendentalist," in *Essays and Lectures* (New York: Library of America, 1983), 208–9.

p. 35–6   Emerson, "Nature," in *Essays and Lectures*, 8.

p. 36   Emerson, "Nature," 10.

p. 37   Emerson, "The Transcendentalist," 208–9.

p. 38   Gilles Deleuze and Félix Guattari, *A Thousand Plateaus*, trans. Brian Massumi (Minneapolis: University of Minnesota Press, 1987), 10.

p. 39   *QPB Science Encyclopedia* (New York: Quality Paperback Bookclub, 1999), 603.

p. 39   Timothy F. Flannery, "Debating Extinction," *Science* 283, no. 5399 (January 8, 1999): 182–83.

p. 41   Eliot, "East Coker," in *Four Quartets* (New York: Harvest, 1971), 29.

p. 41   Eliot, "East Coker," 30–31. Copyright © 1940 by T. S. Eliot and renewed 1968 by Esme Valerie Eliot. Reprinted with permission from Harcourt, Inc.

p. 41   Gary Snyder, *A Place in Space* (Washington, D.C.: Counterpoint, 1995), vii.

p. 41   Snyder, *A Place in Space*, 168.

p. 41   Eliot, "The Dry Salvages," in *Four Quartets*, 44. Copyright © 1940 by T. S. Eliot and renewed 1968 by Esme Valerie Eliot.

Reprinted with permission from Harcourt, Inc.

p. 44   Denise Levertov, *O Taste and See* (New York: New Directions, 1964), 53.

p. 45   Muriel Rukeyser, *The Life of Poetry* (Ashfield, Mass.: Paris Press, 1996), x.

p. 46   Italo Calvino, *The Uses of Literature,* trans. Patrick Creagh (New York: Harcourt Brace Jovanovich, 1986), 98.

p. 47   Alison Hawthorne Deming, *The Monarchs: A Poem Sequence* (Baton Rouge: Louisiana State University Press, 1997), 60.

p. 50   Czeslaw Milosz, *Unattainable Earth* (New York: Ecco Press, 1986), 137.

p. 51   Anton Chekhov, *The Selected Letters of Anton Chekhov,* ed. Lillian Hellman (New York: Farrar, Straus and Giroux, 1955), 57.

p. 55   "Desert Sprawl," *High Country News* 31, no. 1 (January 18, 1999): 6.

p. 55   "Desert Sprawl," 10.

p. 59   Deming, Richard Nelson, and Scott Russell Sanders, "A Call to Action," *Orion* 14, no. 4 (Autumn 1995): 5.

p. 73   John Berger, *Photocopies* (New York: Pantheon Books, 1996), 81.

p. 73   Richard Wilhelm, trans., *The I Ching,*

(Princeton, N.J.: Princeton University Press, 1977), 202.

p. 74   Martha Beckwith, *Hawaiian Mythology* (Honolulu: University of Hawaii Press, 1970), 2.

p. 77   Carl Jung, foreword to *The I Ching,* xxxix.

p. 77–8 Karen Armstrong, "The History of God," lecture from the Chatauqua Institution, National Public Radio, 1996.

p. 91   John Steinbeck, *The Log from the Sea of Cortez* (New York: Viking Press, 1951), 149.

p. 95–6 Henry David Thoreau, *Walden* (Princeton, N.J.: Princeton University Press, 1971), 178.

p. 96   Deming, Nelson, and Sanders, "A Call to Action," 5.

p. 96–7 Deming, Nelson, and Sanders, "A Call to Action," 5.

p. 97   John Dewey, *Art As Experience* (New York: G. P. Putnam's Sons, 1958), 39.

p. 100   Deming, personal correspondence, May 31, 2000.

p. 101–2 Jihyuk Han, "The Poetry of Place: An Interview with Alison Hawthorne

Deming," *Bloomsbury Review* (March/April 1998): 8.

p. 105–6 Deming, *Science and Other Poems* (Baton Rouge: Louisiana State University Press, 1994), 53.

p. 106–7 Deming, *Science and Other Poems*, 70–71.

p. 107 Deming, *Science and Other Poems*, 23.

p. 107 Deming, *Science and Other Poems*, 44.

p. 108 Deming, *Science and Other Poems*, 35.

p. 108–9 Deming, *Temporary Homelands: Essays on Nature, Spirit, and Place* (New York: Picador, 1996), xiii–xiv.

p. 109–10 Deming, *Temporary Homelands*, 200–201.

p. 110–11 Deming, *Temporary Homelands*, 201.

p. 111–12 Deming, *Poetry of the American West: A Columbia Anthology* (New York: Columbia University Press, 1996), xv.

p. 112–13 Deming, *The Monarchs*, 1.

p. 113 Deming, *The Monarchs*, 16.

p. 113–14 Han, "The Poetry of Place," 8.

p. 114–15 Deming, *The Edges of the Civilized World: A Journey in Nature and Culture* (New York: Picador, 1998), 5.

p. 115 Deming, *The Edges of the Civilized World*, 2.

p. 115–16 Deming, *The Edges of the Civilized World,* 22.

p. 116   Deming, *The Edges of the Civilized World,* 206.

SCOTT SLOVIC, founding president of the Association for the Study of Literature and Environment (ASLE), currently serves as editor of the journal *ISLE: Interdisciplinary Studies in Literature and Environment.* He is the author of *Seeking Awareness in American Nature Writing: Henry Thoreau, Annie Dillard, Edward Abbey, Wendell Berry, Barry Lopez* (University of Utah Press, 1992); his edited and coedited books include *Being in the World: An Environmental Reader for Writers* (Macmillan, 1993), *Reading the Earth: New Directions in the Study of Literature and the Environment* (University of Idaho Press, 1998), *Literature and the Environment: A Reader on Nature and Culture* (Addison Wesley Longman, 1999), and *Getting Over the Color Green: Contemporary Environmental Literature of the Southwest* (University of Arizona Press, 2001). Currently he is an associate professor of English and the director of the Center for Environmental Arts and Humanities at the University of Nevada, Reno.

MORE BOOKS ON
THE WORLD AS HOME
FROM MILKWEED EDITIONS

To order books or for more information,
contact Milkweed at (800) 520-6455
or visit our website (www.worldashome.org).

Brown Dog of the Yaak:
Essays on Art and Activism
Rick Bass

Swimming with Giants:
My Encounters with Whales, Dolphins, and Seals
Anne Collet

Boundary Waters:
The Grace of the Wild
Paul Gruchow

Grass Roots:
The Universe of Home
Paul Gruchow

The Necessity of Empty Places
Paul Gruchow

A Sense of the Morning:
Field Notes of a Born Observer
David Brendan Hopes

Taking Care:
Thoughts on Storytelling and Belief
William Kittredge

A Wing in the Door:
Life with a Red-Tailed Hawk
Peri Phillips McQuay

The Barn at the End of the World:
The Apprenticeship of a Quaker, Buddhist Shepherd
Mary Rose O'Reilley

Walking the High Ridge:
Life As Field Trip
Robert Michael Pyle

Ecology of a Cracker Childhood
Janisse Ray

The Dream of the Marsh Wren:
Writing As Reciprocal Creation
Pattiann Rogers

The Country of Language
Scott Russell Sanders

Of Landscape and Longing:
Finding a Home at the Water's Edge
Carolyn Servid

The Book of the Tongass
Edited by Carolyn Servid and Donald Snow

Homestead
Annick Smith

Testimony:
Writers of the West Speak on Behalf of Utah Wilderness
Compiled by Stephen Trimble and
Terry Tempest Williams

Shaped by Wind and Water:
Reflections of a Naturalist
Ann Haymond Zwinger

OTHER BOOKS OF INTEREST TO
THE WORLD AS HOME READER

Essays

Eccentric Islands:
Travels Real and Imaginary
Bill Holm

The Heart Can Be Filled Anywhere on Earth
Bill Holm

Shedding Life:
Disease, Politics, and Other Human Conditions
Miroslav Holub

Children's Novels

No Place
Kay Haugaard

The Monkey Thief
Aileen Kilgore Henderson

Treasure of Panther Peak
Aileen Kilgore Henderson

The Dog with Golden Eyes
Frances Wilbur

Children's Anthologies

Stories from Where We Live—The North Atlantic Coast
Edited by Sara St. Antoine

Anthologies

Sacred Ground:
Writings about Home
Edited by Barbara Bonner

Urban Nature:
Poems about Wildlife in the City
Edited by Laure-Anne Bosselaar

Verse and Universe:
Poems about Science and Mathematics
Edited by Kurt Brown

Poetry

Turning Over the Earth
Ralph Black

JOIN US

Milkweed publishes adult and children's fiction, poetry, and, in its World As Home program, literary nonfiction about the natural world. Milkweed also hosts two websites: www.milkweed.org, where readers can find in-depth information about Milkweed books, authors, and programs, and www.worldashome.org, which is your online resource of books, organizations, and writings that explore ethical, esthetic, and cultural dimensions of our relationship to the natural world.

Since its genesis in 1979 as Milkweed Chronicle, hundreds of emerging writers have reached their readers through Milkweed. Thanks to the generosity of foundations and of individuals like you, Milkweed Editions is able to continue its nonprofit mission of publishing books chosen on the basis of literary merit—of how they impact the human heart and spirit—rather than on how they impact the bottom line. That's a miracle that our readers have made possible.

In addition to purchasing Milkweed books, you can join the growing community of Milkweed supporters. Individual contributions of any amount are both meaningful and welcome. Contact us for a Milkweed catalog or log on to www.milkweed.org and click on "About Milkweed," then "Why Join Milkweed," to find out about our donor program, or simply call 800-520-6455 and ask about becoming one of Milkweed's contributors. As a nonprofit press, Milkweed belongs to you, the community. Milkweed's board, its staff, and especially the authors whose careers you help launch thank you for reading our books and supporting our mission in any way you can.

Typeset in Stone Serif
by Stanton Publication Services, Inc.
Printed on acid-free, recycled
55# Frasier Miami Book Natural paper
by Friesen Corporation.